IMAGES OF ENGLAND

ASHTON COURT

QVI CAPIT CAPITVR

IMAGES OF ENGLAND

ASHTON COURT

ANTON BANTOCK

TEMPUS

For the people of Bristol

Frontispiece: The Coat of arms of the Smyth family who owned Ashton Court between 1545 and 1959. The motto may be translated 'He who rules by the sword shall be slain by the sword'.

First published 2004

Tempus Publishing Limited
The Mill, Brimscombe Port,
Stroud, Gloucestershire, GL5 2QG
www.tempus-publishing.com

British Library Cataloguing in Publication Data.
A catalogue record for this book is available from the British Library.

ISBN 0 7524 3213 3

Typesetting and origination by Tempus Publishing Limited.
Printed in Great Britain by Midway Colour Print, Wiltshire.

Contents

Acknowledgements

I am deeply indebted to: the City of Bristol Museum and Art Gallery for permitting me to publish those portraits now at the Red Lodge Bristol, or in Ashton Court itself, to the Bristol Record Office for permission to reproduce the letter printed on page 61, to Mr Danniels for permission to publish the photographs of the servants on pages 93 and 94, to Mr Tozer for permission to use the rare photograph of the ward of the Red Cross hospital in Ashton Court 1917-19 on page 106, to descendants of the Smyth family and their retainers for allowing me to borrow and copy archive material, to the general public who have been so willing to contribute and share their memories of this precious place and to the Malago Society for all the other material from their photographic archives.

Introduction

Ashton Court is a unique survivor. There has been continuous habitation on this site since prehistoric times. The dimensions of the Great Hall are exactly those of the Saxon log and thatch dwelling that stood on this spot in the sixth century. The building we see today is an intriguing mixture of architectural styles; it seems that every generation that lived here added something without demolishing what had gone before. Grafted onto a medieval manor house are sixteenth and seventeenth century wings – ultimately enclosing two courtyards with embattled gatehouses. Eighteenth century Baroque Regency and Victorian Neo-gothic traditions left their mark, and the result is a puzzle which baffles the experts, but which never fails to charm the beholder with its idiosyncrasies, even in its present half derelict state.

As for the people who lived here, they were larger than life. From their portraits, which were gathered and copied by the Malago Society from private collections all over the world, and their correspondence – a truly remarkable series of letters preserved in the Bristol Record Office and diaries still in the possessions of descendants, their humanity, humour, pathos, and foibles come across the ages with a freshness of an epic film and the directness of Pepys or Tolstoy.

It has not been possible in a book of this type to include anything but a passing reference to the Estate and Long Ashton village, which are inextricably bound up with the great house; for this we must refer the reader to that excellent little publication, *Times Gone By in Ashton Court Estate*, produced by the Heritage Estates Team and available in the Visitor Centre (£1.50). Also see *Long Ashton and Leigh Woods* in Tempus's Archive Photographs Series, and the Domesday entry on Long Ashton. It was then called *Estune*.

For the architecture we recommend *A Thousand Years of Ashton Court* by the Malago Society, whose little pot-boiler *The Inside Story of the Smyths of Ashton Court*, recounting family scandals, legends and ghost stories, is a hardy perennial.

For the definitive history of the Smyth family we recommend Anton Bantock's *The Earlier Smyths of Ashton Court from their letters 1545-1741*; *The Later Smyths of Ashton Court from their letters 1741-1802*; and the three volumes of *The Last Smyths of Ashton Court* (Part 1 1802-1880, Part 2 1880-1900, Part 3 1900-1946). They are published by the Malago Society. The last three are at the knock-down price of £13.00 for the set. Otherwise try the public library.

Long Ashton

according to Domesday Book

Domesday Oak

the Bishop holds Ashton himself

24 HIDES

1 COB

LORD'S DOMAIN 6 HIDES

5 PLOUGHS

14 CATTLE

12 VILLAGERS

10 SMALL HOLDERS

27 SHEEP

7 PLOUGHS

8 VILLAGERS

4 SLAVES

2 COBS

6 SMALL HOLDERS

14 CATTLE

20 GOATS

ONE MILL

Roger the Bursar holds of the Bishop ~ 7 HIDES

20 PIGS

12 PIGS

VALUE £10

36 SHEEP

14 GOATS

Guy the Priest holds of the Bishop 3 HIDES

3 VILLAGERS

2 PLOUGHS

2 SLAVES

VALUE £7

2 COBS

VALUE 100 SHILLINGS

13 CATTLE

2 PLOUGHS

'60 UNBROKEN MARES

2 SMALL HOLDERS WITH 2 PLOUGHS

22 PIGS

80 SHEEP

30 GOATS

The Bishop holds these 3 Manors as one Manor.

According to the Domesday Book, 'three thegns' held the Manor of Ashton before the Norman Conquest. In 1086 the three manors of Ashton were part of the enormous estates in Somerset of Geoffrey, Bishop of Coutances, the builder of the first Bristol Castle. The 'unbroken mares' must relate to his feudal obligation to provide war horses for the King.

one

Early Beginnings

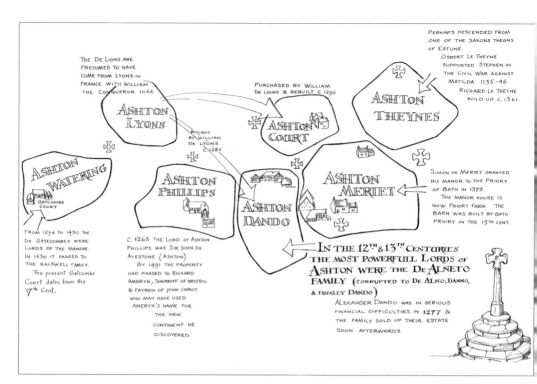

THE DE LIONS ARE PRESUMED TO HAVE COME FROM LYONS IN FRANCE WITH WILLIAM THE CONQUEROR 1066

PURCHASED BY WILLIAM DE LIONS & REBUILT C.1290

PERHAPS DESCENDED FROM ONE OF THE SAXONS THEGNS OF ESTUNE.
OSBERT LE THEYNE SUPPORTED STEPHEN IN THE CIVIL WAR AGAINST MATILDA 1135-46
RICHARD LE THEYNE SOLD UP C.1361.

ASHTON LYONS

BOUGHT BY WILLIAM DE LYONS C.1285

ASHTON COURT

ASHTON THEYNES

ASHTON WATERING

GATCOMBE COURT

ASHTON PHILLIPS

ASHTON DANDO

ASHTON MERIET

SIMON DE MERIET GRANTED HIS MANOR TO THE PRIORY OF BATH IN 1375.
THE MANOR HOUSE IS NOW PRIORY FARM. THE BARN WAS BUILT BY BATH PRIORY IN THE 15TH CENT.

FROM 1296 TO 1430 THE DE GATECOMBES WERE LORDS OF THE MANOR. IN 1430 IT PASSED TO THE HALSWELL FAMILY.
The present Gatcombe Court dates from the 17th Cent.

C.1265 THE LORD OF ASHTON PHILLIPS WAS SIR JOHN DE AYESTONE (ASHTON)
BY 1491 THE PROPERTY HAD PASSED TO RICHARD AMERYK, SHERRIFF OF BRISTOL & PATRON OF JOHN CABOT WHO MAY HAVE USED AMERYK'S NAME FOR THE NEW CONTINENT HE DISCOVERED

IN THE 12TH & 13TH CENTURIES THE MOST POWERFULL LORDS OF ASHTON WERE THE DE ALNETO FAMILY (CORRUPTED TO DE ALNO, DANNO, & FINALLY DANDO)

ALEXANDER DANDO WAS IN SERIOUS FINANCIAL DIFFICULTIES IN 1277 & THE FAMILY SOLD UP THEIR ESTATE SOON AFTERWARDS

Above: In the thirteenth century Long Ashton was divided among several lords. From 1166 the principal lords were the De Alneto family (corrupted to Dando). William de Lyons bought much of the estate from Agnes, the widow of Alexander Alneto, by the year 1303.

Left: In 1390 Thomas de Lyons married Margaret, widow of the wealthy cloth merchant Edmund Blanket. At about this time Ashton Court and All Saints Church, Long Ashton, were rebuilt. The 'refectory' roof, which was probably built in the Guest Wing, is the only surviving feature of this rebuilding.

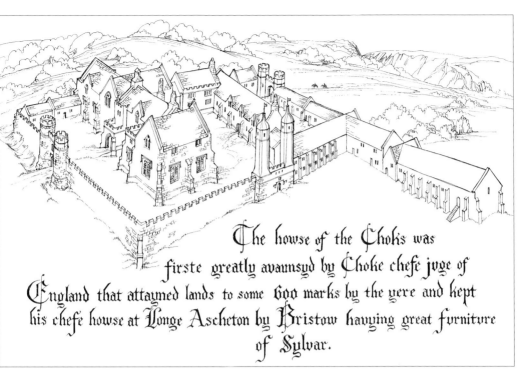

The howse of the Chokis was firste greatly avaunsyd by Choke chefe juge of England that attayned lands to some 600 marks by the yere and kept his chefe howse at Longe Ascheton by Bristow havyng great furniture of Sylvar.

Above: In 1392 Thomas de Lyons obtained from Richard II a licence to 'enclose a park for deer and a warren for rabbits'.

Right: Sir Richard Choke, Justice of the Common Pleas, formerly of Stanton Drew Somerset, acquired the manor of Ashton in 1454. Ashton Court was considerably enlarged by the Choke family. The 'Great furniture of Sylvar', referred to by John Leland in around 1535, consisted of elaborate salt cellars, chalices, ewers and goblets mentioned in Richard Choke's will of 1483 and probably resembled the piece shown here.

In 1506, Ashton Court passed to the estate of Sir Giles Daubeny, soldier and statesman of Henry VII. He had fled the Yorkists after the failure of Buckingham's rebellion against Richard III. He became a privy councillor to Henry VII, Master of the Mint and Lord Chamberlain. He arranged the marriage of Prince Arthur to Catherine of Aragon and crushed the second rebellion of Perkin Warbeck. His son, Henry, succeeded to the estate in 1508. Elizabeth Speke was mistress of Ashton Court around 1537 and Sir John Arundel of Lanherne succeeded in 1541. He led the insurrection against enclosures in Devonshire and was captured and executed at Tyburn in 1549.

In 1545 he sold Ashton Court to John Smyth, a successful Bristol merchant. He was the son of a cooper from the Forest of Dean, who settled in Small Street. John Smyth was apprenticed to a Biscay merchant and subsequently inherited his master's business, wife and ship. He was twice Mayor of Bristol in 1547 and 1554, and died in 1555. His eldest son, Hugh, was a rogue, notorious for his brawls, insulting behaviour, harbouring ruffians, abusing his authority as JP, ill-treating his servants, extortion and forgery. His raid on Sir George Norton's deer park in 1579, in which one man was killed, was brought before the Star Chamber. He died in 1580.

The following portraits adorned the walls of Ashton Court until the great sale of 1947 dispersed them to private collections all over the world. A few were acquired by the City Museum and Art Gallery and are also displayed in the dining room at Ashton Court and in the Red Lodge, Bristol. A few others, including the Samuel Cooper miniatures, went to the Cottrell-Dormer family in Rousham.

Left: Matthew Smyth was the partner in crime with his brother until marriage to an heiress brought him respectability and wealth. He became a much esteemed lawyer of the middle temple. He died in 1583.

Right: Jane Tewther boasted blood of the Kings of Leon and Castille and connections with the Tudors. She was a capable manager, adding to the estate and upholding feudal rights with vigour.

Helena von Snakenborg was the daughter of a Swedish nobleman who came to England in the train of King Eric XIV of Sweden, one of the suitors for the hand of Elizabeth I. She became a maid of honour and a personal friend of the Queen. Colt Hoare of Stourhead relates the amusing story of how Sir Thomas Gorges, a courtier of Elizabeth I, proposed to Helena. He invited her to a complicated dance and tripped her up, and they both crashed to the floor. Next day he appeared with a ruff round his right knee. The inquisitive Queen asked him the reason. 'This knee had the honour to get between the knees of your beautiful maid of honour, Helena von Snakenborg'. The Queen roared with laughter, 'Never mind, Sir Thomas, keep trying and perhaps you will get both knees in the same position'. Sir Thomas proposed and was accepted. They built Longford Castle on the proceeds of a Spanish galleon wrecked on the Hampshire coast, given to them by the Queen. Their daughter, Elizabeth, a god-daughter of the Queen and named after her, was married to the second Hugh Smyth of Ashton Court.

The second Hugh Smyth was knighted by James I in 1611. He became a courtier and entertained Anne of Denmark in Bristol in 1613. He shared an interest in race horses with Prince Henry and Prince Charles. He drove hard bargains and had a reputation for meanness and misanthropy. Elizabeth wrote to her son, 'Here come not any but such as are sent for, and coler doth much abound with us, as ever it did. God increase my patience to endure it still'. Hugh died of the bloody flux in 1627.

ELIZABETH ELDEST DAUGHTER
OF SIR THOMAS GORGE AND
LADY NORTHAMPTON, MARRIED
SIR HUGH SMYTH KNIGHT

Elizabeth Gorges was a beautiful and virtuous lady. To her son Tom, aged twelve, she wrote, 'I hope Mr Betty took measure of you ... that, when he makes you winter clothes, they may be big enough. I know that you will have a care to keep yourself as warm as you may. When the cold weather comes in – remember your neck and feet. Thy most loving and careful mother, Elizabeth Smyth.'

14

THOMAS SMYTH ESQ.R SON OF SIR HUGH SMYTH, KNIGHT.
MARRIED FLORENCE ELDEST DAUGHTER OF JOHN LORD POULET
HE WAS ELECTED TO PARLIAMENT FOR THE COUNTY OF
SOMERSET THE 30.th MARCH, 1640 AND DIED OCTOBER 1642.

Thomas Smyth is in his 'long clothes'. He was a child prodigy and was sent to St Johns College, Oxford, at the age of twelve.

FLORENCE POULETT,
DAUGHTER OF JOHN,
FIRST LORD POULETT AND
WIFE TO THOMAS SMYTH ESQ^r

The 'Inigo Jones' wing. Thomas Smyth had witnessed the building of the Banqueting Room of the Palace of Whitehall and, it has been alleged the same architect was engaged by him to box in the Tudor Long Gallery at Ashton Court with a neo-classical façade in the 1630s. It is unlikely that Inigo Jones was involved. The windows are not symmetrical because they reflected earlier openings. The Jacobean balustrade was retained and a corner buttress survives from an even earlier period.

Opposite: Florence Smyth was a daughter of John, First Lord Poulett of Hinton St George. She was a child bride at fifteen. To her husband, aged seventeen, she wrote, 'Mr Smith, I must entreat you to send the coach on Monday for me, for all their coaches will be so full that I cannot have a roome in any of them, and besides there's nobody will be willing that the coach that I shall go as fast as the coach must go that I go in...' She was later a devoted wife and mother.

JOHN, FIRST LORD POULETT, BY CATHERINE DAUGHTER OF HENRY, LORD NORREYS, BARON OF RYCOT, MARRIED CHRISTIAN DAUGHTER OF CHRISTOPHER KENN ESQ.^{R} DIED MARCH 20th 1649.

John, First Lord Poulett, the principal magnate in Somerset. He was an outspoken critic of Charles I, yet championed the Royal cause in the Civil War. He was on excellent terms with his son-in-law, Thomas Smyth. 'Sonne Smith,' he wrote to Tom, 'Pray send me down ... a pair of socks to play tennis in: ye size of your foot will serve for ye length...' John, First Lord Poulett was forever looking in his chamber pot to diagnose what ailments he was suffering from. He served in the Bishops War from 1634-40, fought with Tom at Sherbourne in 1642 and took part in the siege of Exeter. He died in 1649.

Col. Thomas Pigott. When Thomas Smyth died of smallpox in Cardiff on 2 October 1642 aged thirty-two, his widow was courted by an Irish knight with Roundhead sympathies. She married him in 1647 and they moved to Brockley Court, where she began a second family – the Smyth-Pigotts. Col. Pigott was understandably not popular with his 'in-laws', who referred to him as 'Ffatt brother Pigott'.

Hugh Smyth Bart. The third Hugh Smyth was the rising hope of Cavaliers in the West Country between 1655-60. He plotted for the return on Charles II and, after 1660, was rewarded with a Baronetcy. He was an active JP, served as MP for the county in 1665, and was Colonel of the Militia and Deputy Lieutenant. He was resolute in compelling the Bristol Corporation and Dissenters to bow to the Royal will. He died in 1680 aged forty-seven.

John Ashburnham was the father of Ann Smyth and Groom of the Bedchamber to Charles I and Charles II. His devotion to Charles I in his escape from Oxford in 1646 and Hampton Court Palace in 1648, led to a prolonged spell in the Tower and three banishments to the Channel Isles. He was restored to favour in 1660 and was a shrewd diplomat and very often a power behind the throne.

Ann Smyth, née Ashburnham, from a miniature by Samuel Cooper. She was a pathetic, helpless creature, ill–used and neglected by her husband. She never enjoyed good health and coughed so much that she once split the front of a bodice, '...I have had the spleen to a violent degree: it broke the lace of my wasecot in two...' Nevertheless she had six children and lived to be over eighty.

At the restoration Ann Smyth wrote to her husband, 'There is to be miti doings at Bristol – the condits are to ron wien [run wine]. I doubt my mother-in-law [Florence Smyth Pigott] will be quite disgrast – she wod not be porsweded to it, so I send a barril of sider'. In 1663, Charles II brought his barren queen, Catherine of Braganza, to Bath, in the hopes that the waters would help her conceive an heir. Lord Ashburnham wrote to Hugh that the Royal Physicians had urged the King to drink asses' milk, and would he take two asses from Ashton and deliver them to one of 'the pages of the back stayres'. Later Charles II rode over to Bristol and visited Sir Hugh at Ashton Court.

Uncle Amyas Poulett was Hugh's uncle and he was infatuated with Hugh's wife. To his 'dearest lady, your very very very owne adorer', he pours out his soul, his misfortunes, his frenzied drinking bouts, local gossip, ailments, his 'peeping about for a wife' and his mustering of the local militia – mostly Somerset country bumpkins, in a flow of prose equal to his more famous contemporary, Samuel Pepys. He died unmarried in 1669 aged forty-seven.

Colonel Romsey was a soldier of fortune, a rogue and a villain. He became an agent for Hugh Smyth and married his widow. Always short of money, he deliberately fomented plots against Charles II and his Catholic heir, James, in order to expose his accomplices at the last moment for hard cash. By turning informer, several prominent men were executed for alleged complicity in the Rye House Plot of 1683. Romsey was arrested and kept in prison till 1688 – he evidently knew too much. His wife 'fell into convulsion fits', but outlived him by nine years.

John Smyth, the son of Hugh, was a squire, sheriff and MP. He was decorous, dull, devoted to his family and undistinguished. He had an obsessive fear of smallpox and was touchy and misanthropic. This increased on the death of his wife in 1715. After that, his daughters referred to Ashton Court as, 'This Nunnery at Ashton'. He died in 1726.

Elizabeth Astrey. 'Betty' was vivacious, affectionate and superstitious (she once went to a witch in Bedminster to help her find three missing silver tankards). Her 'horrid scrauls' to her husband, John Smyth, are full of local gossip and household matters, and are apologetically signed 'a dull, simple grunting creature'. Totally desolated by her husband's long absences in Parliament, she filled her time making 'babyclouts' for her numerous family. She died aged forty-three.

Left: A monument to Betty Smyth at Long Ashton church.

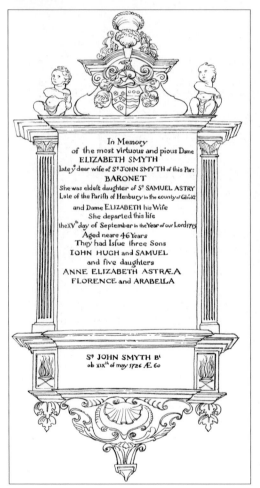

In Memory
of the most virtuous and pious Dame
ELIZABETH SMYTH
late y^e dear wife of Sr JOHN SMYTH of this Par:
BARONET
She was eldest daughter of Sr SAMUEL ASTRY
Late of the Parish of Henbury in the county of Glou^r
and Dame ELIZABETH his Wife
She departed this life
the XVth day of September in the Year of our Lord 1715
Aged neare 46 Years
They had Issue three Sons
IOHN HUGH and SAMUEL
and five daughters
ANNE ELIZABETH ASTRÆA
FLORENCE and ARABELLA

Sr JOHN SMYTH B^t
ob XIXth of may 1726 Æ. 60

THE HOLY
BIBLE,
CONTAINING
The Old Testament
AND
THE NEW:
Newly Translated out of the Original Tongues,
AND
With the former Translations diligently Compared and Revised.

𝕭𝖞 𝕳𝖎𝖘 𝕸𝖆𝖏𝖊𝖘𝖙𝖎𝖊𝖘 𝕾𝖕𝖊𝖈𝖎𝖆𝖑 𝕮𝖔𝖒𝖒𝖆𝖓𝖉.

Appointed to be Read in Churches.

LONDON,
Printed by *Charles Bill,* and the Executrix of *Thomas Newcomb,* deceas'd;
Printers to the Kings most Excellent Majesty. MDCCII.

Anne Smyth was born the 24th of October 1693.
a little after fiue in the morning. died unmarried—

Elizabeth Smyth was born the 8th of December 1696.
at ten at night. died unmarried

Astræa Smyth was born the 15th of January 1697/8
at four in the morning. married to Thomas Cooter Esqr.

John Smyth was born the 24th of July 1699.
at eight at night. twice married no issue sine exitnet

Florence Smyth was born the 2 of August 1701.
a little after four in the morning. married Jarritt Smyth Esqr.
Issue.

Arabella Smyth was born the 21st of March 170 2/3
between 3 & 4 in the afternoon. married Ed: Gore Esqr. Issue

Hugh Smyth was born the sixth of March 170 5/6
about eight in the morning. died at Banow unmarried

Samuel Smyth was born the first of April 1708 School
about half an hour after two in the afternoon. died at

September the fifteenth 1715 It pleas'd God Almighty out of
his infinite mercy to take to him self my most dear Wife after a
painfull sickness that lasted her five months, she was one of the
very best of Wives, the best of mothers, the best of friends and
the best of Christians, she has left me and her eight children
behind her, who can never condole enough the loss of such a Wife
and such a mother, and one that left such a bright example of piety
and vertue and every thing thats praise Worthy for us to follow.
The Lord grant that I and my children may live Godly, rightous and
penitent lives whilst on earth, that we (with her) may be pertakers
after this painfull life ended of everlasting joys thro' the only merits
of Our Lord and Saviour Jesus Christ Amen.
                                            John Smyth

The family Bible was given to Sir John by his wife in 1702. In it was recorded the year, the day and the hour of the birth of their eight children. Sir John, who never appreciated Betty when she lived, was inconsolable when she died. The family Bible is now at Rousham, Oxon.

Opposite right: The frontispiece of Sir John's Bible.

Above: Elevation of Ashton Court, 1695.
Below: Panoramic view from the south west, *c.*1730.

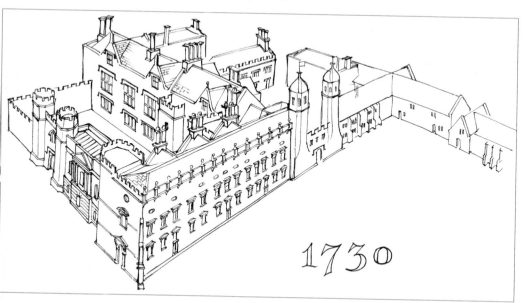

1730

Opposite: John Smyth – 'Profligate Jack'. The second Sir John was charming, talented, versatile and generous. He was much in demand at house parties because he could sing and accompany himself on the spinet. His extravagancies reduced the estate to ruin. His marriage to two commoners and failure to produce an heir was a disaster for his house. He died 1741.

Florence Smyth was one of four co-heiresses of Sir John Smyth II. She first married John Pigott who died of gaol fever and secondly Jarrit Smith. She had six children by Jarrit, but only two survived infancy. She did not enjoy good health. To Jarrit: 'I have been extreem bad since Saturday afternoon I am so fainty I can hardly live...' She relied heavily on her three sisters, Arabella Gore, Astrea Coster and Anne (Nancy) who never married.

'Nancy' was very much her mother's favourite. She was 'mother' to many younger brothers and sisters when Betty died. Anne never married. Her father rebuilt Bishopsworth House for her, but she chose to live at Henbury House, where she dedicated herself to good works. She died in 1761.

Jarrit Smith was of humble origin; his father was a Worcestershire soap-boiler. He became a successful businessman and solicitor and was an MP for Bristol from 1756 to 1768. He carried the bill for the rebuilding of Bristol Bridge and was presented at court in 1760. He lent considerable sums of money to Sir John Smyth II. He married his sister and co-heiress. On settlement of debts he gained possession of Ashton Estate in 1741. Later, he bought half of Arabella's share from her son, John Gore. In 1763 he received a Baronetcy. He adopted the arms and the name of Smyth. He died in 1783, aged ninety-one, leaving a prosperous estate and a copious and largely undecipherable correspondence. He is the only member of the Smyth family whose portrait, which was hanging in Ashton Court until 1947, has not been traced.

Jarrit Smith was an entrepreneur extraordinaire; everything he touched turned to gold. He was the first to develop the Bedminster and Ashton Vale coalfield, which became a major source of income to the Smyth family in the nineteenth century. He owned part-shares in several merchant ships, notably the *Blandford* and the *Tiger*, which in the many wars against France and Spain brought in handsome prizes.

John Hugh Smyth, who was the eldest
son of Jarrit, was meticulous, scholarly
and philanthropic, but like his father
was a hard-headed businessman and
singularly lacking in humour. He was
Captain of the Militia from 1759 to
1762, a founder member of the Theatre
Royal Bristol and a benefactor of the
Bristol Royal Infirmary. He had strong
antiquarian interests and patronised the
historians, William Barrett and John
Collinson. He was also a zealous fox-
hunter. He died heirless in 1802.

Elizabeth Woolnough was a wealthy
heiress from Pucklechurch and she
brought considerable fortune to the
Smyth Estate in the form of a sugar
plantation in Jamaica, which was run
with slave labour. She was an eccentric
and capricious lady; she gambled and
hunted with reckless abandon, took a
perverse delight in doing the opposite
of what her doctor recommended and
lived to a cantankerous old age. She
retired to Clift House in Bedminster on
the death of her husband and opened
Coronation Road in 1820. She died in
1825.

WILLIAM BARRETT, F.A.S.

SURGEON,

AUTHOR OF THE HISTORY AND ANTIQUITIES OF BRISTOL.

Ætatis 51.

William Barrett was a successful surgeon and a friend of Sir John Hugh and his brother, Thomas. He was encouraged by John Hugh to write the first comprehensive history of Bristol, but was sadly gullible enough to include a number of spurious stories leaked to him by a naughty schoolboy called Thomas Chatterton. When the truth came out, the critics tore his book to shreds and poor Barrett died of chagrin. Revd John Collinson was given the living of Long Ashton by Sir John Hugh in order to write the monumental work, *The History and Antiquities of the County of Somerset*, the first comprehensive compilation of local archives and the starting point for all local historians. The strain of his labours proved too great and Collinson collapsed and died in 1793, aged thirty-six.

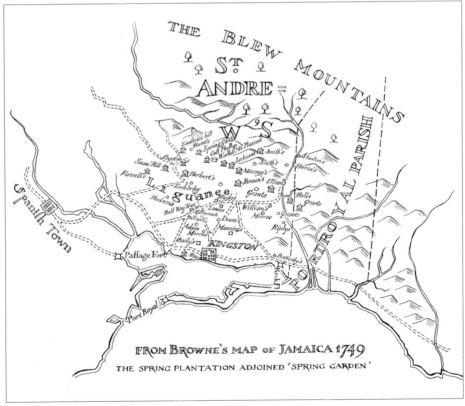

FROM BROWNE'S MAP OF JAMAICA 1749

THE SPRING PLANTATION ADJOINED 'SPRING GARDEN'

Above: Sir John Hugh appointed Humphrey Repton to draw up plans for the remodelling of the east front of Ashton Court, facing Bristol. Repton's plans, which included a gatehouse, an octagonal kitchen, an Elizabethan keep and an elaborate oriel window in a romantic neo-gothic style, would have transferred the main entrance from west to east, with a distant view of Bristol docks, which was the source of much of Sir John Hugh's wealth. But his death in 1802 prevented this plan from being carried out.

Opposite above: Sir John Hugh wrestled for nearly fifty years (1757-1802) with the problems of running a sugar plantation in Jamaica. In spite of enormous difficulties of communication, dishonest agents, hurricanes, slave insurrections, wars, loss of sugar through delays, faulty loading and the problem of sharing the estate with an unsatisfactory part-owner, Colonel French, the Spring plantation actually made a profit and he bequeathed a massive fortune to his nephew and heir, Hugh, who wisely sold the plantation before emancipation ruined the planters.

Opposite below: The Spring Plantation lay twenty miles inland from Kingston, among the foothills of the Blue Mountains.

John Hugh's nephew and successor, Hugh, was the eldest son of his younger brother, Thomas Smyth of Stapleton. Thomas was a country gentleman-farmer. He inherited the Smyths' Gloucestershire estates, was a trustee of the local turnpike, a commissioner for sewers and supported the Pittite candidate for Bath. His account book records '8s 8d for negus gloves and turnpike' to take his wife to Bath where they played cards and enjoyed a little polite society. He records, 'To John for mending my breeches 7s 10d. To Nottsway for mending my wig 4s 0d.'

Thomas Smyth married the heiress Jane Whitchurch and, when her father died, he inherited his property and fortune, with which in 1784 he re-built Heath House in Stapleton. He shared a love of music with Jane and 'paid Mr Thompson for Violin book and strings etc. £3 14s 6d' and 'to Harding for mending my fiddle 2s 0d'.

Four children, whose births were attended by Dr Barrett, survived infancy: Florence born in 1769, Hugh born in 1771, John born in 1774 and Mary born in 1776. Three of these in turn succeeded to the Smyth Estate.

Hugh Smyth, the eldest son of Thomas of Stapleton, succeeded his uncle, John Hugh, in 1802. He was a wilful, insolent young man and had fallen out with his father when he was a student at Oxford because of his extravagance and debauched lifestyle. He was a fanatical huntsman. He dissipated his uncle's fortune, building ostentatious new stable wings at Ashton Court (now the restaurant and visitor centre) and remodelling much of the west front in a vaguely mock Elizabethan style.

Elizabeth Howell was the daughter of the harbour master at Loughor and a companion of Hugh's mother, Jane. He had got Elizabeth with child, but was forced to put her aside and marry Margaret Wilson, the daughter of the Bishop of Bristol, who was the bride chosen for him by his uncle, who had great expectations of him. Needless to say, he soon abandoned Margaret and went back to Miss Howell.

Left: On the death of Margaret, Hugh married Miss Howell, but neglected to have his son John Hugh legitimised. He therefore could not inherit the Smyth Estate. However, this son married a Smith-Pigott heiress, whose estates included Brockley and most of Weston-Super-Mare. Weston's elegant stone streets were laid out by John Hugh Smith-Pigott when the arrival of the railway in 1844 launched it as a popular seaside resort.

Below: Among Hugh's extravagances was a magnificent silver table, (now the showpiece of the museum of Sheffield plate in Sheffield). One of his more disreputable habits was to tip-toe up behind Miss Emmins, a lady he engaged to play the organ, and drop a home-made stag beetle down the front of her bodice. He was certainly not a gentleman.

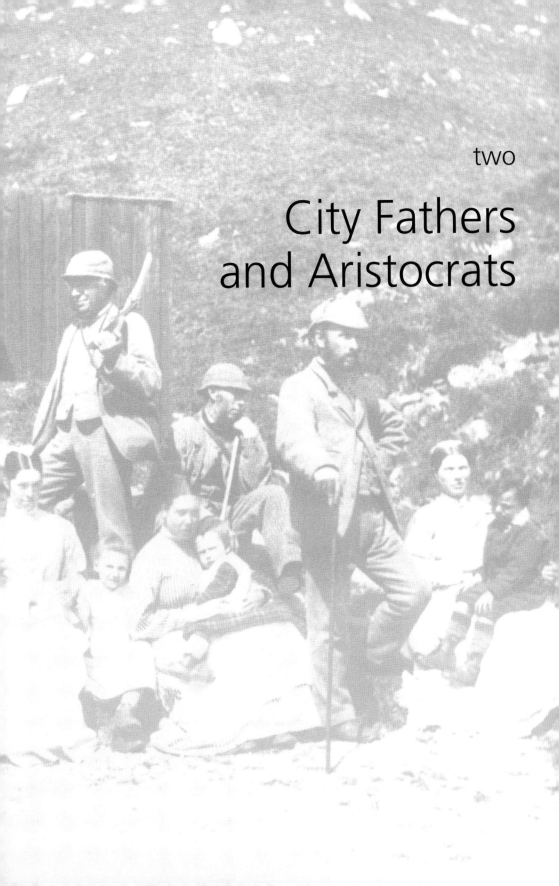

two

City Fathers
and Aristocrats

Above: The east front of Ashton Court as it appeared around 1810, showing the fine perpendicular window, which still survives in the Inner Hall. This courtyard was enclosed when Sir Hugh Smyth built the new stable block and it was given a conservatory style glass and girder roof by Greville Smyth around 1885, to make a winter garden. The roof was removed and the fifteenth-century kitchen and service wing on the right were demolished in the 1960s and this area is now the bar.

Opposite above: The south front showing part of Sir Hugh's new stables *c.*1810. The baronial gatehouse was raised to its present height in 1873 and the windows of the stables were considerably enlarged when Sir Greville Smyth converted them into his museum around 1884. The perpendicular window (right) was assiduously copied in the remodelling of the west front (*c.*1810).

Opposite below: The west front as it appeared after 1810, showing the copied perpendicular window inserted in the Huntsman's Hall, the Great Hall and Grand Staircase.

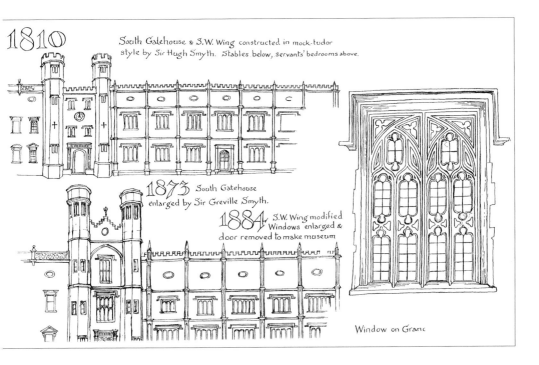

1810 South Gatehouse & S.W. Wing constructed in mock-tudor style by Sir Hugh Smyth. Stables below, servants' bedrooms above.

1873 South Gatehouse enlarged by Sir Greville Smyth.

1884 S.W. Wing modified Windows enlarged & door removed to make museum

Window on Granc

Left: Sir Hugh Smyth's elder sister, Florence. Edward Gore wrote to Thomas of Stapleton, 'my love to my cousin Florence, and tell her she must not put more than half a pound of powder on her hair at one time, which is the fashionable quantity', and a little later he wrote, 'Why don't Florence marry? I want my cousins to spread: the more Good Houses the better to visit.'

Below: At last, in 1799, when she was thirty, Florence married John Upton of Ingmire Hall, Westmorland. They had one son, Thomas Upton.

Mary was the youngest of Thomas Smyth's children. John Read, a college friend of her brother, Hugh, writes, '...I never see a black bug or spider but I think of little Mary, to whom Captain Manley sends his best respects, and hopes the turban she wore at Bath last winter is perfectly safe...'

In 1798, Mary married Col. Benjamin Way, the eldest son of the Squire of Denham Place, Buckinghamshire, and had ten children.

As Sir John Smyth III, who succeeded his brother Hugh to the Ashton Court Estate in 1824 was a confirmed bachelor, Florence Upton and Mary Way were next in line and, to make doubly sure, Florence's son Thomas was married to Mary's second daughter Eliza. The gamble paid off. They became the parents of Greville Smyth, the last Baronet of Ashton Court (1836-1901).

Sir John Smyth III who succeeded to the Estate in 1824, was a solitary and somewhat sinister individual. He preferred the company of his bloodhounds and shunned human society, because, it was said, he suffered from an unfortunate complaint which caused him to smell very offensively. He was an adroit businessman; he developed the Bedminster and Ashton Vale coalfield, bred pedigree cattle, surrounded his park with a seven-mile wall and built two of the gatehouses in Clerkencombe and the lawn or City Gate (now in the grounds of Ashton Park School).

Sir John died in 1849, partly from the shock of having received the day before, a visit from a gentleman claiming to be his nephew, Richard Smyth, son of Hugh by, it was alleged, a secret marriage to one Jane Vandenburg in Ireland in 1798. The lady died in childbirth, and the child's existence was kept a secret because Richard alleged his father was obliged to marry Margaret Wilson. If this was true then Richard, not his uncle, John, should have been the owner of the Ashton Estate. Sir John, in some alarm, rashly promised the entire estate to Richard. His two sisters, Florence Upton and Mary Way who were now both widowed, saw the prize slipping from their grasp and, it has been suggested, administered something to their brother to put him out of the way, before Richard Smyth could make good his claim. Mary died in 1850 but Florence Upton was by then an alarming and dotty old woman of eighty and moved into Ashton Court. She died three years later and the estate descended to her younger grandson, John Henry Greville Upton, a minor of sixteen, who on his majority changed his name to Greville Smyth.

During Greville's minority 1852-1857, his uncle, Arthur Way, was steward at Ashton Court. It was during this stewardship that Richard Smyth with his solicitor, made a second visit. After listening to them patiently for an hour, Arthur Way ordered the male servants to grab them by the wrists and ankles and throw them out. Richard, claiming to be the rightful owner, circulated the tenants telling them to pay their rents to him and not to Arthur Way. He threatened to take Ashton Court by storm and Arthur Way had policemen stationed round the park wall armed with muskets and swan shot.

The claim of 'Sir Richard' was finally demolished at the sensational trial, 'Smyth *v*. Smyth', in August 1853 at the Gloucester Assises. 'Sir Richard' was exposed as an impostor called Thomas Provis, who had been in prison for stealing horses. Provis claimed to the end that he was a Smyth, 'because all males of the House of Smyth are born with a pigtail'. He was sent to gaol for life; but survived just long enough to publish his story *The Victim of Fatality*.

Jane Vandenburg was alleged by 'Sir Richard Smyth' to be his mother. In fact, the lady in this miniature is unknown; the name Vandenburg was claimed because it appeared in the family Bible he had bought in a bookshop and in which he had forged the record of his parents' marriage and the signatures of those who had witnessed it. Two wills of Sir Hugh – leaving the estate to Richard – were also found to be forged, and also various heirlooms on which the family motto 'Qui Capit Capitur' was wrongly spelt 'Qui Capit Capitor'.

Thomas Upton of Ingmire Hall was the son of Florence Smyth. He was the heir to the Ashton Court Estate but died young of pneumonia in 1843, after riding over the moors from Ingmire to Kendal in foul weather to pay the Upton rents into the bank. The claim passed to the second son, Greville.

Eliza, the wife of Thomas, was one of the ten children of Mary Way. Marriage to her cousin, though bad for the genes, ensured that the estate eventually came to their offspring. Eliza was a cheerful, sensible soul, with a sense of the ridiculous, which bubbles forth from the diary she wrote at finishing school in Paris between 1824 and 1828.

Thomas Upton Junior was the eldest son of Thomas and Eliza Upton. He was an intelligent youth, who wrote a *History of British Vampires* and was infatuated with Jenny Lind. On the death of his father, he was sent to his crazy old grandmother, Florence Upton, in Bath, who indulged his every whim. He took to drinking, gambling and riding so recklessly, that he was seriously injured and died of delirium tremors in 1848 at the age of eighteen. There is a monument for him from his grandmother in Long Ashton church, recording untruthfully his many virtues.

John Henry Greville Upton inherited the Ashton Estate at the age of sixteen. With his mother and sister, he took up residence in 1854. He was deeply attached to the Upton home in Westmoreland and was never happy in the West Country. He was painfully bashful and played no part in public life. He even paid a fine rather than serve as Sheriff, which was an honour expected of him by the city of Bristol.

Florence Upton was high spirited, intelligent and good looking and was Greville's youngest and favourite sister. She married Clement Cottrell Dormer of Rousham (Oxon) and had fourteen children whom she brought up single-handedly, owing to the early death of her husband. She kept a remarkable journal, which is the principal source for the history of Ashton Court in the Victorian Age. She died in 1907, aged seventy.

Fanny Upton was another of Greville's sisters. She was a pretty girl, but fell head first downstairs while attending a private school in Clifton and suffered splitting headaches all her life. Any noise brought on a fit of 'screaming horrors' and for the rest of her life she had to be rushed from one watering place to another by elderly relatives. She died unmarried in 1876.

Above: Of their early days at Ashton Court from around 1854 to 1856, Florence wrote in her journal, 'my brother was very fond of dancing and, as there was a deficiency of partners, the servants used to be summoned to the mazy dance to the sound of the great organ – I very much disliked dancing Sir Roger de Coverley with a footman'.

Above: The Hotel Victoria, Promenade des Anglais, Nice, was the first halt on George Oldham Edwards' honeymoon tour. Probably by design, Greville and party joined them there where they were presently joined by his mother and sister, Florence. Florence wrote in her diary, 'About one, Greville came in, very glad to see us, as we were to see him, looking so remarkably well. Soon afterwards Emily came in. She had been married rather more than a fortnight and looked pale'. What the diary does not tell us, though it was known among the family, is that during that Italian honeymoon, Emily and Greville conceived a helpless passion for each other.

Opposite below left: Emily Way was the eldest of the eight very good looking children of the Revd H.H. Way. She had an alabaster complexion, eyes like sapphires and hair like spun gold. She came to be known as the 'loveliest woman in the West of England'.

Opposite below right: But Emily was lame as a result of a childhood illness and this was considered a deterrent to desirable suitors, so the first time a gentleman showed interest, her father rushed her into a loveless marriage. Her husband, George Oldham Edwards of Redland Court, was many years her senior and was the Director of the Old Bank. At her wedding in Henbury church in 1856, Florence Upton was one of twelve bridesmaids dressed in crinolines and pale blue archery caps with plumes. Greville, who was too shy to declare his love for the cousin he had long admired, in a fit of pique, left the country with his tutor and college friends for the 'Grand Tour'.

This page: The three parties continued their voyage southwards to Florence, Siena and Rome, where they united for sight-seeing and socialising. On 13 April, they ascended Vesuvius, with the ladies on chairs. George Edwards felt giddy and demanded to be taken back and, compensated the chair bearers by distributing 'the contents of his brandy bottle between them far too freely', as Florence wrote. 'Greville walked up and we found him on the edge of the crater enveloped in sulphurous smoke. Oh! What a fearful place it was to look down, awful rumblings and rattlings were going on beneath, and the smell of the sulphur stifling...' On the way down she fell off her donkey, 'and had to be picked up. No damage done'.

Opposite below: The day ended with the lighting of a monstrous bonfire measuring 40ft high and 111ft in circumference and an imposing firework display given by the celebrated pyrotechnist, Professor Burn. So with a bursting of jerbs (fireworks), jets of golden rain, and crimson sky rockets, recurring discharges of artillery, the clanging of church bells and singing of 'God Save the Queen', Greville Smyth came into his majority.

Above: On 2 January 1857, Greville came of age. The day began with a twenty-one gun salute from the top of Ashton Hill, followed by the pealing of bells from all the city church towers. Some 500 tenants and their families in their Sunday best made their way to Ashton Court beneath triumphal arches inscribed with the words 'Welcome to the Home of thy ancestors'. At the west door the young baronet was hoisted onto a cider barrel and the tenants drank his health. Greville replied, promised to be a good landlord and treated them to a slap–up dinner in a marquee.

With a private income of £27,000 a year, Sir Greville Smyth spent most of the year travelling the empire. It was the age when it was considered an aristocratic virtue to hunt and kill anything that moved. Greville shot bucks and bulls in India, buffalo in North America, crocodiles in Egypt and kangaroos in Australia. Only in his later years did he begin to take a scientific interest in the species he was so indiscriminately slaughtering.

His companions on many of these hunting forays were his old tutor, Thomas Jeans, 'who lived abroad for reasons of economy', and a few college friends.

Here is Greville in Egypt around 1868, with Thomas Jeans, his travelling physician Dr Frederick Holmen, and two pretty Way cousins. Greville made at least four excursions up the Nile, usually on his way to his favourite hunting fields, the jungles of Ceylon.

Above: During his brief visits to Ashton Court, he frequented the Bristol Races on Clifton Down. This photograph shows his party setting out from the west door with a number of companions in an enormous travelling carriage. Greville faces left with one foot on the rear wheel. Inside was his uncle, Henry Hugh Way, the vicar of Henbury. Waiting in the porch, and one of the party was Avena Blackburn, the daughter of the vicar of Long Ashton. Between two footmen George Lloyd and George Liston, on the right is Mr Curtis, the butler.

Right: Greville indulged in a mild flirtation with Avena, who was good company but large-limbed and bovine. She was a competent horse woman and certainly fancied herself as mistress of Ashton Court. Greville loaded her with presents, cloisonné boxes from China and, on one occasion a sulphur-crested cockatoo from Australia. When, years later, Greville married his beloved Emily, Avena returned the cockatoo and, in a fit of peevishness, married one of her father's choirboys, Frank Corbett, who was many years her junior and quite definitely not her class. Avena is the lady on the right.

The first photographs of Ashton Court were taken in 1866 by a Long Ashton sugar merchant, William Ravenhill Stock. The west front today remains structurally unchanged. Only the magnolia trees have grown.

The west front from the drive shows an unfamiliar avenue of elm trees, dating from the eighteenth century. These had disappeared before 1900, but young trees took their place around 1995.

The south front before the Baronial Gatehouse was rebuilt in a more grandiose style in 1872. The entrance to the stables can still be seen in the fourth bay from the right. The whole of the south lawn was a formal garden with geometrically arranged flower beds until after the First World War.

Above: The parterre and rose garden before Greville planted the giant redwoods, which in 2004 obscure the house from this angle.

Opposite below: Greville's mother and sister, Florence, are at Erchless in 1858. Another guest was Clement Cottrell-Dormer from Rousham Park, Oxon, 'and whilst he was there', writes Florence, 'our marriage was talked of. My mother, however, would not hear of its taking place for many months, though he was permitted to give me a ring." It was, of course, an arranged marriage, proposed by the mothers of the parties concerned, who had been close friends since Eliza's schooling in Paris from 1824 to 1828. The marriage took place in Long Ashton church on 27 April 1868. It turned out to be singularly successful: she had fourteen children in rapid succession, who in the absence of an heir to Ashton Court, naturally had great expectations.

Above: In 1857, Greville, like many of the English aristocracy, followed the example of Queen Victoria and Prince Albert, by spending much of the year in the Scottish Highlands. For some twenty years he rented Castle Erchless, an inconvenient old peel tower, from the Chisholm Clan in Glen Cannich. From August through to Christmas, he kept an open house for his hunting pals, and very often his beautiful cousin, Emily Edwards and her father. This is a watercolour of Castle Erchless. Unfortunately the deer, the fox and the salmon were not the only things pursued in the Highlands. It was almost certainly here that, in November 1862, she fell pregnant. Esme was born in August 1863 and was always officially 'Esme Edwards', the daughter of George Oldham and Emily Edwards of Redland Court, but there can be little doubt that Greville was her natural father. Her only son Greville Edwards, born in November 1856 – after the honeymoon she shared with her husband and cousin in Italy – must also raise doubts about his paternity.

Left: Greville is at the window with binoculars with friends at Erchless, *c*.1875. All guests were expected to write verses in Greville's visitor's book. These, ranging from the sublime to the ridiculous, were later privately published in *The Book of the Glen*. Omitted from the published edition were poems about the gentlemen's binoculars trained on lady guests bathing naked in the loch, when they should have been looking for game.

Sometimes Greville took his cronies up to a cottage beside Loch Mullardoch. Here they are striking a pose with crofters wives. In the absence of sport, if we are to believe *The Book of the Glen*, the most debauched drinking bouts took place here.

'Sunday Nov 1 1868. Damp, thirsty and blowing. Liquor all round. Beetles, flies, etc., as before. Curious quantities of rats and mice constantly running under the door and out the window. Fruitless pursuit. Liquor all round to console us. News of deer. Tommy goes in pursuit. Wish him luck in the usual manner. General loss of appetite at lunch. Liquor allowed to fill up the vacuum. Tommy returns remembering it's Sunday. Commend his scruples and celebrate the event. Grev' finds curious dog under the table, black with yellow tail and ears. King finds another in his bedroom, green picked out in red. Celebrate both events. Festive evening. Turn in early. Sunday a remarkably thirsty day. Grev', King, Tommy, Digger and all the dogs in the bath.'

Greville Smyth in his prime. He was quite short in stature and distinctly portly in middle age. The thick chestnut hair receded and turned white. He never lost his chronic reserve, which was acute in society or in the presence of women. On the death of his brother-in-law, Clement Cottrell-Dormer, he was frequently summoned by Florence to correct and discipline her unruly sons.

Florence Cottrell-Dormer and her family at Rousham in 1880. From left to right standing: Charlie aged nineteen, Miss Bodley with William aged one, Beatrice aged twenty, Miss Stephenson with Kitty aged two, Aubrey aged five, Hilda aged ten. From left to right sitting: Clem aged sixteen, Flo aged seventeen, John aged twelve, Clement, Florence, Max aged eleven, Winny aged three. Two other children, Dorothy and Greville, died as infants. Florence was pregnant with Humphrey when this photograph was taken and he was born on 29 April 1881, four months after her husband died of heart failure, aged fifty-three.

Ashton Court,
Clifton, Bristol

5th of February

Sir

I have the honor to inform your Royal Highness - that the total bag at Tickenham - on 30th of January including the Pheasants picked up on the two following days

is as under

Pheasants	603
Partridges	1
Woodcocks	3
Hares	7
Rabbits	7
Total	621

We were very fortunate in having a fine day on Wednesday - as it rained in torrents

Thursday & Friday

I am
Sir
Your obediently
Greville Smyth

The letters exchanged by Greville Smyth and the Prince after the event are formal to the extent of coldness. George Oldham Edwards had died in 1883, and it was common knowledge that both men were interested in his beautiful widow. The Prince had met her previously when he had made a formal visit to Bristol, when Edwards had been Sherriff. Greville got in first and married Emily in April 1884, but, if we are to believe the gossips, HRH was permitted to have his way with her on a fairly regular basis. Local people still talk of the secret venues, mostly cottages in the neighbourhood which were used as a rendezvous.

Opposite above: In January 1884, the Prince of Wales made a private visit to Greville's neighbour, Philip Miles, at Leigh Court. Greville was one of the party and Philip suggested that Greville might like to entertain the Prince and his party at a shoot at Tickenham. Greville dutifully received the Royal guest and arranged for a seven-course picnic luncheon at Hales Farm. The official photograph shows Greville seated in the centre, no doubt at the request of HRH, while he the guest takes up a position on the extreme left.

Opposite below: Another photograph of a group of Greville's friends relaxing after a shoot at Tickenham, by William Ravenhill Stock, November 1880. The area is still called 'the Wild Country'. From left to right: -?-, Greg Way, son of Greville's Uncle Arthur Way, who had been steward of Ashton Court from 1852 to 1857, -?-, -?-, Ashton Court agent, Tom Dyke, who had played a big part in developing Smyth land in Bedminster, (an area originally called 'Greville Town' which is now Greville Street and Greville Road), Greville's old friend, the soldier of Empire Sir Redvers Buller VC, Mr Jere Osborne, a distant relative. The 'bag' for the day can be seen on the ground behind them and at a respectful distance in the rear are the beaters, looking like characters from Dickens.

On the death of George Oldham Edwards, aged sixty-nine, in 1883, Florence wrote, 'We all wondered what would be the next event in the family'. The announcement of Greville's marriage to Emily in April 1884 surprised nobody, '...long expected: come at last: Mr Jeans [Greville's old tutor] prophesied dreadful things: their tempers would never suit, she would make him jealous and there would be scenes...' Florence totally opposed the match. In the normal course of events she, or her numerous family, could expect to inherit the Smyth fortunes. And here 'she was at Claridges Hotel with all her presents and her daughter Esme,' whom everyone guessed was Greville's child and heir. 'As I had for years disliked and snubbed the lady, she repaid this with interest and hardly ever asked us for more than two nights at a time and very seldom that. So that Greville, after his marriage hardly knew my children by sight. She made him a better wife than anyone expected and they were happy together. She was, I believe, the love of his life.'

Left: The evening before, Greville wined and dined the old Erchless fraternity for the last time at Cox's Hotel, Jermyn Street, London.

Opposite below left: 'Tettie's Bonnet', along with 'Mrs Edwards' wedding dress', found its way into the society magazines of the time. 'Tettie' was Emily's niece, Henrietta Way (née Ross) the wife of her brother Wilfred.

Opposite below right: 'Greville loaded her with jewels, as he had done for many years', wrote Florence sourly, and the *Western Daily Press* published a list of these in breathtaking detail, '...blue turquoise and diamond bracelets, emerald and diamond ring, turquoise and, diamond ring, diamond and sapphire ring, diamond and emerald square locket, etc.'

Left: Both Greville and Emily were forty-nine at the time of their wedding. Florence's opinions of the arrangements were predictably jaundiced: 'a worse managed wedding I never was at, no-one had given any orders for seats to be kept and so shop girls and milliner's apprentices rushed in and filled every pew. We, the wedding party, had to stand the whole time and were ready to drop. I think some crawled onto the pulpit stairs and sat there. A dreadful scene of crush and crowd and a sad scene to me in many ways.'

Mrs Edwards
requests the pleasure of
Major & Mrs Wilfred Way's
Company on the occasion of
her marriage with
Sir Greville Smyth
at St Georges Church Hanover Square
on Thursday April 24th
at ½ past 3 o'clock.

At Home at Claridges Hotel, Brook Street
at 4 o'clock.

R.S.V.P to Claridges Hotel

After a honeymoon of eighteen months hobnobbing with high society in half of the spas and resorts of the old Europe, Greville brought Emily home to Ashton Court. The famous yellow carriage was waiting for them at Temple Meads and they swept down Coronation Road, lined with 1,200 Bedminster schoolchildren. Near St Paul's church, a platform had been raised; the carriage stopped and a small child presented Emily with a bouquet in which the word Bedminster had been picked out in tiny blue flowers.

Above: Part of Emily's baggage was her daughter Esme. At twenty-one she was a tall, imposing girl, who was less good looking than her mother, but much more talented. She was outgoing, adventurous and much less constrained by the snobbish middle-class attitudes of her mother. She had an affinity with animals, especially reptiles. She once climbed into the snake pit at Bristol Zoo and allowed them to coil themselves around her.

Above right: The estate workers manhandled the carriage up to the west door of Ashton Court, where the same fulsome toasts that had been first uttered at Greville's coming of age, a quarter of a century before, were repeated; except that this time Emily added, 'I shall make it my first duty to make my husband stay in Ashton and take an interest in his estate.' This was a pious wish. Greville continued travelling for most of the year with Emily and her entourage, on a much more lavish scale. The local press trotted out lengthy tributes.

Above: During Greville and Emily's honeymoon, Major Davis, a fashionable architect, was engaged to 'victorianise' Ashton Court. The central courtyard was roofed in to make a conservatory or Winter Garden, with tropical shrubs, reminiscent of the Ceylon jungle. This was approached through an elaborate fan-vaulted hall. The Grand Staircase, with magnificent newel posts, was rebuilt. Sir Hugh Smyth's stable wing of 1810 was converted into a museum to house Greville's growing collection of zoological specimens.

Right: Two immense chimney pieces were inserted into the museum in French Renaissance style with the quaint inscriptions, 'Welcome as is the Spring to Earth' and 'A hundred thousand Welcomes'.

The decor of Ashton Court in the Emily era represented the height of Victorian bad taste. Good seventeenth- and eighteenth-century portraits were banished in favour of sentimental farm-yard scenes by George Moreland. The Long Gallery was given a mock Jacobean plaster ceiling and was cluttered with *fin de siècle* bamboo and rush armchairs, Japanned cabinets, Indian octagonal stools, massive German musical boxes, majolica library chairs, bear and leopard skin rugs, and tiger skins.

In the museum, which was formerly stables, birds and creatures shot or trapped by Greville were stuffed and arranged in naturalistic and usually savage poses in magnificent mahogany cases. In his later years, Greville began to take a scientific interest in the game he had so recklessly slaughtered: he learnt how to stuff birds and animals and began to classify the specimens. Finally, a large bungalow was built at the top of the park (which is now Redwood Country Club and Hotel) for the overflow collection.

The Great Hall is the oldest part of the house, and is the exact dimensions of the Saxon Hall on this site. By 1885 it reached its ultimate metamorphosis, crammed with a plethora of tasteless bric-a-brac from almost every century.

The Winter Garden was Greville's pride and joy. All that art and science could do, was combined here to recreate a tiny corner of the Ceylon jungle in what had been a medieval courtyard. Here he and Emily played host, sat in their wicker chairs, drank tea and planned their journeys.

Greville sits for his photograph on the occasion of a rare visit from his sister Florence
Cottrell-Dormer and (to his left) two of her daughters, Beatrice (standing behind looking
left) and Flo (to Greville's right). Florence looks resigned and disagreeable, probably because
on these occasions Emily feigned illness and retired to sulk in her boudoir. The photograph
was taken beside the fountain in the sunken garden where Greville's redwoods were
beginning to shoot upwards.

Emily's boudoir was a dream of feminine delicacy and refinement. Alternating panels of
tapestry and bevelled plate glass mirrors concealed spacious cupboards for her extensive
wardrobe and even a bath, though the water had to come and go in enamel pails. Except for
the massive marble seventeenth-century fireplace, it could have been a first-class cabin on
the *Titanic*.

Tea in the Winter Garden photographed by Esme, *c.*1895. Greville stands behind Emily. To their right is Admiral Bythesea VC and his wife Fanny Belinda. To their left is Charlie Cottrell-Dormer, his wife Ursula, and far right, Cecil Irby. Charlie said on returning to Rousham, 'The butler suddenly burst in and announced that the first footman had tried to get into bed with the head housemaid. "Just fancy," exclaimed Fanny, "It might have been me!" ' This was wishful thinking perhaps; she had married an old husband and had no children.

The appointment of suitable servants was the responsibility of Edgar Way, the house steward, who is seen here (to the left) in his study with his daughter, Dolly. He was a widower, and a former P&O purser; he had a walrus-like moustache, a flirtatious manner and a penchant for all things naval. This may explain why he dressed Dolly in naval uniforms and required her to salute him. She was rather square, mannish and odd and, with the passing of the years, she became odder.

In August 1890, Greville's oldest nephew, Charlie Cottrell-Dormer, married Ursula Cartwright of Aynho Hall, Northamptonshire, at St Paul's, Knightsbridge. 'Greville and Emily sat near us, the former in great spirits', wrote Florence. Emily's sulks may be explained by the fact that, in the absence of a legitimate heir, Greville's fortune might one day go to Charlie and not to her daughter, Esme.

Ursie Cartwright is in her wedding dress. Florence found her an unsatisfactory daughter-in-law. She was argumentative and unpunctual and, though she bore Charles three sons, it was not a happy marriage and it ultimately broke up.

Six months later, in January 1891, Esme married Gilbert Irby in Long Ashton church. Esme had expressed her opinion fairly forcibly on the subject. She wanted to marry a captain in the Anglo-Indian army, who was apparently willing to reciprocate. The 'Pater' and Emily, in some consternation, consulted their old friend General Redvers Buller VC. 'Good Lord no', exclaimed the General, 'he's a rotter – don't let your daughter marry him'. 'Alright', snapped Esme, 'I'll marry anyone you like.' In fact, the officer condemned by Buller was not the one she had in mind, but by then it was too late. Her parents had chosen another and Esme never got the man she wanted. These photographs were taken in the West Indies during their honeymoon tour. Esme looks very bad tempered.

The husband selected for Esme was Gilbert Irby, the third son of Lord Boston, Greville's old hunting companion from Hedsor, Buckinghamshire. Gilbert was dark, slightly built, with a drooping moustache and hair parted in the middle. In his youth he had had a learning difficulty. Until the age of ten he refused to speak and, his family believed he was deaf and dumb. When he suddenly held forth they were astounded. This may account for the pronounced drawl and excruciating slowness with which he ate his food and why he could not sleep at nights unless he wore earplugs and patches over his eyes.

In 1894 Esme and Gilbert made a honeymoon voyage round the world. Esme took her box camera and tripod. Her studies of shipboard scenes, colonial society and native life reveal her enterprise, energy and flair for photography and rare talent for composition.

The voyage took them to Capetown, then New South Wales and New Zealand. The long haul across the Pacific and up the east coast of South America was taken on board SS *Ruapehu*.

Esme assembled crew and passengers for this picture. They look superbly sure of themselves in a world in which the British were then undoubtedly the masters.

The carpet goes down the companionway to the first class cabins. People of Esme and Gilbert's class could expect a degree of luxury when they travelled and internal arrangements ensured that the classes were rigidly segregated.

Even the contents of Gilbert's holdall on the wall above his bunk are perfectly identifiable.

The satin-wood panels, stuccoed ceiling and fittings of the saloon were not appreciably different from the hotels of the period. The piano and well-thumbed magazines are some indication of long sea voyages of that period.

At Wollongong, south of Sydney, Esme and Gilbert went to visit her cousin Hilda (née Cottrell-Dormer), who had married Alexander Dundas Robertson. Despite appearances, the Dundas Robertsons were facing hard times. Through unwise speculation their finances were in ruins and the estate was heavily mortgaged.

Hilda's tiny waist and leg of mutton sleeves must have been excruciating in the Australian summer heat. She had more success with her parrots than with motherhood.

Hilda and Alex Dundas Robertson are in the four-wheeled wagonette, probably posing for Esme's camera.

An interesting study by Esme, who also photographed, with her father in mind, stuffed koala bears, aboriginal boomerangs and a duck-billed platypus.

On a previous voyage, Esme and Gilbert had made the acquaintance of the King of Fiji, who begged them to visit his islands. At that period, the gentry touring the empire had no difficulty finding a welcome from resident British judges, administrators, governors and missionaries and, of course, a familiar cluttered drawing room with chintz curtains and knobbly furniture.

Contact with the natives, who had been cannibals twenty years earlier, was limited to assembling the 'domestics', who include an Ayah, or a native nurse, holding Mrs Somerville's baby.

It probably took some nerve in 1894 for a white woman to confront these Fijian natives with a box camera and tripod.

Esme and Gilbert rounded Cape Horn but did not go ashore at Rio de Janeiro. Even so, Esme's studies of the familiar skyline – before its statuary but with three-masted ships at anchor – are full of period atmosphere.

Coaling, a necessity for long sea voyages of this period, was always tiresome for the passengers. The noise and dust, as natives scrambled aboard with coal for the engines, made sleep impossible.

The Dining Saloon on the SS *Ruapehu* had fixed wooden seats, serge cloth, and potted plants. In the tropics punkahs were fixed up above the tables and jerked manually to stir the air.

Nothing conveys better colonial society in the heyday of the British Empire than Esme's superb study of a tea-party for the governing white elite with the native servants standing deferentially in the background. This was probably in Jamaica.

Mr MacTurk was a geologist living up-country in British Guiana. His house is typical of the colonial homes of this period. The living rooms were raised well above ground level to catch sea breezes and the kitchen wing was practically detached to reduce the danger of fire.

In this delightful study one can almost identify what Gilbert and Mr MacTurk had for their picnic.

1890

And How I Spent the First Five Months.

IT was a dull, dark morning, on January the 14th, 1890, that a small party met at Charing Cross Station to witness the departure of the mail-train to Dover. Two ladies and a gentleman had already taken their seats, and were bidding adieux to a circle of friends who were crowding round the carriage door. 'Good-bye; mind you write soon!' a few hearty shakes of the hand, the whistle sounds, pocket-handkerchiefs are waved, and the train glides slowly out of sight.

I must now explain to my readers who we are and where we are going. Firstly, I, the writer, had better describe myself as a fair, middle-aged lady, by name Emily Smyth, about to start on a trip to Ceylon and Egypt with my

Greville and Emily also travelled widely in the British Empire in the 1890s. With them went Dr Holman 'medico' and, sometimes Esme and Gilbert. Emily wrote a short book about the journey in 1890, published privately for the benefit of her brother, John Way, who was meant to have travelled with them but could not because of ill health. It is the travel experience of a rich bored woman, who even had a live cow carried in their special train as far as the French Riviera, so that she could always have fresh milk.

Greville, Emily, Dr Holman and Gilbert are all visibly wilting in the heat while posing for Esme in front of the Taj Mahal, with the whole place presumably emptied of native 'riff-raff' for the event. If Emily was overcome with the flies or the heat, she always had Greville to fan her and the 'medico' to read to her. Even on the Ceylonese railways, she had only to clap her hands and chilled champagne was immediately available.

Opposite below: Their favourite hill station was Nuwara Eliye in Ceylon. Emily imposed upon the 'medico' to write whole chapters of her book and illustrate it with his sketches when she grew bored with it. The Grand Hotel where they stayed was little more than a glorified bungalow, but Emily kept up appearances by engaging four coolies in pink turbans and pink cotton knickerbockers to run her about in a rickshaw. Once, taking a corner too fast, they tipped her out. 'There she was', quoted Florence Cottrell-Dormer, who accompanied them on this occasion, 'out in the road; some English people passing stopped to help; and some natives ran up, one with a glass of water. She escaped with frightful bruises and general stiffening. On our return, Nicholas (her man) hit the coolie and knocked off his turban'.

Above: Greville and Gilbert, carried aloft by porters, are armed with butterfly nets. They are going to add to the huge collection of trapped, stuffed and impaled lepidoptera in the museum at Ashton Court. This must be somewhere in the Ceylonese jungle.

Greville and Emily spent the last five months of each year in Scotland – in enormous rented castles large enough to accommodate an indoor staff numbering thirty or more, not to mention large numbers of guests. From 1887 to 1897, they rented Ardross Castle in the Black Isle. Greville wanted to buy it, but the owner, a sauce manufacturer, refused to sell. Greville, is with some of his guests at an Inverness studio. Standing to his left is his cousin Henrietta Way (née Ross) and seated is Eliza Cotten Prior, one of the jolly daughters of his Aunt Louisa Prior, who had kept house for him at Ashton Court after his mother died in 1870. Sprawled rather stiffly at her feet is John Smith Osborne, who married her in 1875.

In 1898, Brodick Castle on the Isle of Arran was rented. In 1899 and 1900 Penninghome in Wigtonshire was also rented.

Finally, in 1901, Thurso Castle, perched on the northernmost extremity of Scotland, was rented. The more impractical and inaccessible the better; the domestic and travelling arrangements could be left to others. It was at Thurso Castle on 28 September 1901, that Sir Greville Smyth died of bronchitis. His end may have been hastened by a fall. He was sixty-five.

Sir Greville Smyth and Emily Smyth
in their later years (*c.*1890) from
portraits in the possession of the City
of Bristol Museum and Art Gallery and
now hanging in the dining room at
Ashton Court.

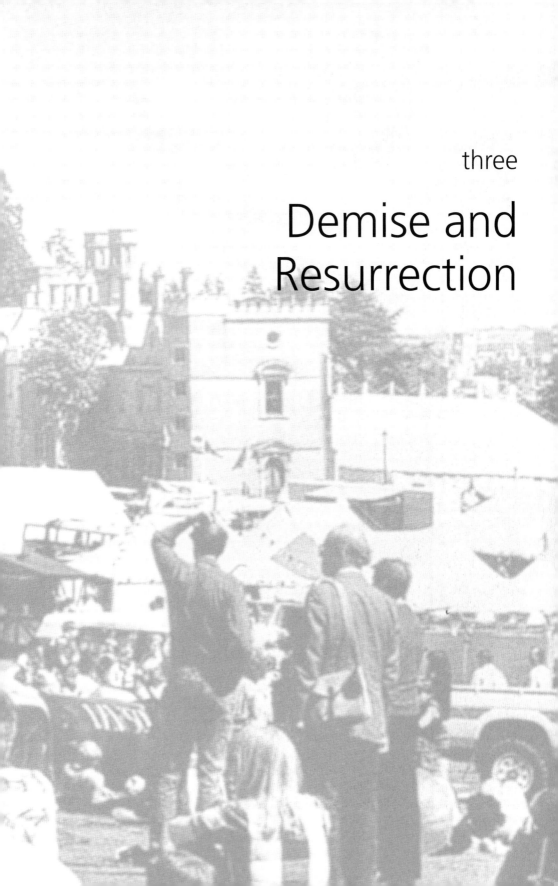

three

Demise and Resurrection

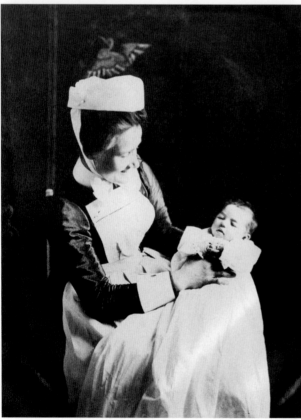

This page
Above: Six months before
Greville's death, his only grand-
child was born. After ten years of
marriage, on 24 February 1901,
Esme gave birth to a daughter –
Sylvia Frances. It was a difficult
birth and the pregnancy
aggravated a morbid condition of
Esme's legs, brought about by the
misuse of iodine when she was a
child. She was laid up for weeks
after with inflamed veins and was
still on crutches in September.

Below: Esme showed scant interest
in Sylvia. A second child, Eileen,
only survived a few hours. She
wanted a son and her only interest
in Sylvia was as a convenient
subject for her tripod and camera.

Opposite page
Above: Emily is in her canary-
coloured carriage at the west door
of Ashton Court *c.*1905.
Throughout the Edwardian era,
Emily was a familiar figure,
hobnobbing with the gentry in
the boulevards of Clifton. When
her special train arrived or
departed from Temple Meads
station, the stationmaster in his top
hat and tailcoat was always there
to bow her in and out of her
carriage.

Below: An amazing study by Esme
of Emily (extreme right) and her
sisters in the Winter Garden,
Ashton Court *c.*1905. Left: Mrs
Maria Grote-Joyce ('Murdie' or
'Fat Lumps'). Standing: Miss Alice
Way ('Taff') and centre: Mrs
Isabella Way ('Issy') of Denhom
Place, Uxbridge.

Left: Dame Emily, as she preferred to be known after her widowhood, was much in demand in these years, opening fêtes, flower shows and laying foundation stones. Here she is surrounded by wasp-waisted ladies and whiskered worthies opening a church fête at Stanton Drew around 1907.

Below: Dame Emily was very much the 'Great Lady' of Long Ashton between 1901 and 1914. When the Long Ashton Cricket Eleven played a home match, she would have her carriage wheeled onto the edge of the field and send her butler over to bring villagers to talk to. The church parade was positively feudal. The entire congregation stood until 'milady' and her entourage were seated in the family pew and, on her return she would throw 'largesse' to the crowd – mostly silver 6d and 3d pieces. Not a voice demurred. The entire village and far beyond depended on her entirely for their tenant farms, jobs, tied cottages and charity.

The Gentlewoman.

The Illustrated Weekly Journal for Gentlewomen.

No. 62.—Vol. III.
(Registered as a Newspaper, and for transmission abroad.)

Saturday, September 12, 1891.

Price Sixpence.
(By post, Sixpence-halfpenny.)
All Copyrights reserved.

Idyll of the Hour.

❦ ❦ ❦ ❦ ❦

A Too Fanciful Fancy.

Let us be a wee bit historic. Let us, if you do not mind, *mes amis*, take a walk back, or a little stroll back, into the last century. In the days of powder and pomander and patches, what did the fashionable higher cult most indulge in? I mean, in courting the goddess Pleasure, or rather in trying to banish Monotonous Boredom. Tired of Chinese monsters, Chelsea pugs, dragon-plates, basto and quadrille, our dainty ancestresses took up with mysticism. Do you remember Scott's pretty story of " My Aunt Margaret's Mirror," and how in the days of the great Marlborough, and when wits were at their wittiest, and there was yet plenty of sensation in the way of sensational news, yet the necromancer had a capital time of it. A prophetic mirror was quite the sensation of the whole of Edinburgh. Again, later on, was there not the far-famed Cagliostro, and was there not Monsieur Mesmer, and they were the "modest " of the mode : I don't mean timid or backward, but that they were only too forward in some of their impostures. Again, too, was there not a good deal of mysticism, what with his affinities—elective affinities—and I don't know what, about the great Goethe.

Mysticism has always been the mode at some time or the other. We have our cycles of it. In the tussling times of war in the beginning of the present century, and for a little time further on, we did not hear quite so much about it ; but now, good friends, tired of the season's crush, of the country tennis, or when Aix les Bains and Homburg and Trouville grow to be hollow mockeries, what is there to fall back upon, what fanciful fancy? Well, a little mild esoteric Bhuddism, or Theosophy, or thought-reading, or something of that sort. But do you not think that we might take up with something perhaps healthier? Folks who live honest, good lives, without too much history in them—happy the life without a history, even as a State—very sensibly, indeed, trouble themselves but little about the supernatural, nor are they for ever analysing each other, and the why and the wherefore of everything. They take the world as Bulwer Lytton recommended, as it is, and make the best of it. They don't think about thinking, nor feel about feelings, and try to see about seeings, and so on. There are more things than we know of in our philosophy. Very likely. Perhaps they are just as well left alone.

My dear sister Theosophist, I do not wish to say anything unpleasant to you or about you. " Have each his creed," said the great novelist and satirist in his quaint rendering of Beranger. Everyone is entitled in a free country to think as she likes. Be mystic, then, and have letters and communications of all sorts by telephone or from other worlds. But, *eh bien*, do you know that you might amuse yourself a little more wisely? There are plenty of things worth thinking about in the actual world. Charity begins at home. Worry yourselves, my dear friends, less about the Bhuddist firmaments and more about doing your duty to those around. For my part, I am rather sorry to see a really intellectual woman take up with a new fad, or even sometimes with a new faith. Let us drop the theosophy of the tea-table and be healthy. Please pardon this sermon.

❦ ❦ ❦ ❦ ❦

"THE GENTLEWOMAN" AUTUMN FASHION DOUBLE NUMBER will be published on Thursday, October 1, at the usual price of Sixpence, under the title of " Autumn Leaves." It will contain, as well as its ordinary features, the very latest fashions in Gowns, Millinery, Coats, Jackets, Cloaks, &c., &c., charmingly illustrated in colours, and will, in its entirety, be a number quite unique in its many attractions. It should be ordered at once.

Gentlewomen "At Home."

❦ ❦ ❦ ❦ ❦

No. LXII.

Lady Smyth at Ashton Court, Clifton.

High on a hill over beautiful Avon, sheltered by ancient trees from the gaze of the modern world, yet in view of its loveliness, stands an old time manor-house—dating onward from the thirteenth century. The glamour of

Lady Smyth.

dead and gone years still hangs in the air, and here indefinably co-exists with the luxurious environment of these later days. Long and long ago, when the Lions ou de Lions, in the far back olden time emigrated from Lyons, "a province in France," and in 1287, after the Norman Conquest, roved along the southern coast of the newly subjugated island, they saw in the parish of Long Ashton a sunny spot which seemed good in their eyes. And so these men of old, being in quest of a beautiful valley, pitched their tents where wooded hill, and smiling vale, and rippling stream, and dashing waterfall were crowded close by Nature's lavish hand. And here they turned the soil and drove into the earth the first stakes of a tent,

destined to remain while many dynasties were born, flourished, and tottered to their fall. Part of the present mansion was erected by those sturdy knights of yore, and in the left wing, which contains the oldest part of the house, there is a quaint oaken door, opening off a broad gallery, which leads into a little casemented room, and this is called Drax's Kennel, because of its appropriation in old days by an ancient huntsman who rejoiced in the name of Drax. An adjoining tiny door with three steps leading up to it reveals a narrow twisted passage, dimly lighted by two of the oldest up and down little windows, and here is The Fox's Hole. Why, nobody knows, but the name remains if the legend is lost. Perhaps, *qui sait*, a mediæval Reynard hard pressed for shelter by oncoming foes, bethought himself of a certain succulent pantry—not unknown in times of peace—where he might once again console the inner fox, and lie *perdu* from the hungry fangs of ruthless hounds or the equally inconsiderate shafts of sporting archers.

The Deer Park was enclosed as far back as the second Richard's reign, and still sends fawn and buck to the Ashton larders. One John Smith was living at the Court when Henry VI. was King of merry England, and then the estates passed from Sir Thomas Arundel, and have since remained with his descendants. The front of the mansion was rebuilt by Inigo Jones in 1633, and had he lived the entire house was to have been remodelled. However, *Dieu dispose*, and so the changes were left for other hands. The present owner, Sir John Henry Greville Smyth, succeeded to the property on the death of his grandmother, Mrs. Smyth, in the year 1852, and in the April of 1884 married his cousin, Emily Frances Way, daughter of the Rev. Henry Way, of Alderbourne Manor, Bucks, and the subject of our present sketch. Lady Smyth had previously married the late Mr. George Oldham Edwards, of Redland Court, Gloucestershire, and had by him two children—a son and daughter.

As can be seen from her portrait, Lady Smyth both has been and is possessed of great personal beauty. Deep blue eyes shining with a sweetness of expression which trebly enhances their natural charm, golden hair waving and luxurious, lightly touched with grey, and a complexion absolutely flawless now—must have been, when Lady Smyth was twenty, " A sight to make an old man young ! " But loveliness of face and form, however complete in itself, is without the higher beauty an imperfect quantity, and it is in the large charity of Lady Smyth's kindly soul, and her infinitely practical benevolence, that the gracious charm of her presence most influences those who know her. A friend of many years writes :—" One does not know when to end telling of her goodness and, indeed, it is impossible to say too much. The almswomen, the children, and the very old are Lady Smyth's chiefest care ; and her carriage may often be seen stopped on the roadside, while she chats long and cheerily with some ancient goody or tottering old man, who has worked 'man and boy ' on the estate, and now in declining years is gently thought for and remembered by his beloved mistress."

Lady Smyth's great work is the Convalescent Home at Long Ashton for women, and there is a touch of pathos in its history which irresistibly appeals to all who hear it. When only five years old, Lady Smyth, through the carelessness of a nurse, contracted a slight lameness which has lasted through her life ; but the trial was turned to good account. If she could not dance she could at least help others back to life and strength ; if there was to be no tennis, no skating, no Swiss mountains to be " done," there were other heights to climb, and loftier. So this trouble—if trouble it was—brought forth only tender sympathy with those less richly blessed in the good things of this world, and when Lady Smyth married

A somewhat fulsome tribute in a fashionable magazine of 1891, to Emily Smyth's charity, notably her convalescent home for distressed gentlewomen.

91

On the occasion of the Golden Wedding of Revd John Way of Henbury. who was Emily's brother, there was a reunion at Henbury Vicarage for the entire Way clan in 1910. Esme assembled them on the lawn for this magnificent photograph. Dame Emily, who was lame and almost blind, can be seen in the centre and her grand-daughter, Sylvia Irby, sits at her feet.

Dame Emily Smyth opened the fourth day of the Brislington Fayre in 1913. Her silver-headed black bamboo cane was inscribed 'Lady Smyth Ashton Court Bristol' and was dated 1907. It surfaced recently in a sale and has now been returned to Ashton Court.

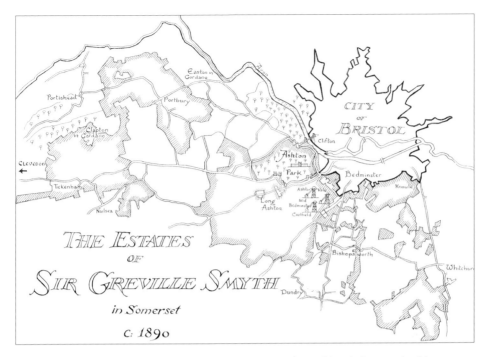

The lavish lifestyle of Sir Greville Smyth and Dame Emily could only be sustained by frequent sales of land to the growing city of Bristol. This erosion of their capital assets was accelerated by a decline in farm rents, industrial troubles in the coal pits, super-tax, tax on land values and death duties. A large number of farms were sold in 1917 and the estate finally crashed in 1946.

The indoor staff at Ashton Court are assembled and photographed by Esme c.1910. None of these people can be identified with any certainty. The heads of departments, namely the cook, the butler, the housekeeper and lady's maid, took their meals apart from the other servants, who were suitably deferential to them.

Above: The butler, two footmen, pantry-man and hall-boy are at the west door, together with two estate workers, *c.*1898.

Left: John Wilkinson the hall-boy is seated between the two footmen. Whatever their real names were, the first footman was always called William and the second Arthur, to avoid confusion. Evening wear for footmen was black trousers, a light blue cut-away coat with solid gold buttons, a stiff shirt with a white bow and a yellow and black striped waistcoat.

Right: When she was middle-aged, Esme Irby began putting on a lot of weight and gained in height and width. Also, her hair started falling out, which was later to be reinforced by her long since discarded girlhood tresses. At about this time, she indulged in an erotic correspondence and probably a relationship with a lady who addressed her as 'Darling Coltie' and signed herself 'your loving Jockey' with a drawing of a whip. Here is Esme in a perfectly ghastly court dress in around 1906, with Sylvia, who seems to have had a thin time of it.

Below: Sylvia, who was well chaperoned by a lady's maid and gentleman relative, was allowed to visit the Long Ashton School children, who had been instructed to make nesting boxes.

They also made beehives. It is most unlikely that anything approaching the most innocent familiarity with 'village' children was permitted. Mr Gunston was the Head Teacher. Three of his four sons, all of whom appear here, were killed in the First World War.

At Christmas the children from Long Ashton School went up to the Winter Garden in Ashton Court to sing carols for Lady Smyth.

A great number of beautifully posed studies by Esme exist of Sylvia, some of which are of exhibition standard. Sylvia shared a love of pets with her mother, but was surrounded by servants and was not permitted any friends of her own age. There is no doubt that she was desperately lonely much of the time.

Sylvia is on the steps at Ness Castle, Inverness. First rented, then purchased, this building became, for many years between the wars, Esme's favourite home.

Left: Sylvia is with 'Hilly'. Miss Kate Hilder was Esme's lady's maid and chaperone to Sylvia for much of her childhood.

Below: Esme had begun to surround herself with Pekinese, bulldogs and parrots and these were only marginally less important to her than her daughter. Letters from Sylvia to her mother, while she was at boarding school around 1912, detail how she would cry out from the nursery wing at Ashton Court, 'Mumsie, oh mumsie, please take me with you', cries which went largely unheeded. She only got the same old boring ride in the governess cart.

After 1910, Esme began to take Sylvia 'to spa', mostly at the Hotel Excelsior Aix-les-Bains, along with many other rich people, who tried to soak off the layers of fat which were the normal result of over-indulgence during the London Season.

Sylvia at a society event, *c.*1910. There are numerous rich and titled ladies, but no children except for Sylvia.

This fragment of a photograph shows Sylvia with 'Gan-Gan' and some of the indoor staff, *c.*1912. By this time, Dame Emily was almost continuously confined to a wheelchair and was rapidly losing her sight.

Opposite above: Emily and later her daughter Esme, handed over, by degrees, the whole of Greville's enormous collection of stuffed birds, animals, butterflies, birds' nests, eggs, seashells and everything else, to the City Museum and Art Gallery. These were displayed in the magnificent mahogany cabinets made especially for them. In 1930, two rooms entirely dedicated to their collection, the 'Sir Greville Smyth Room of Natural History' and 'Dame Emily Smyth Room of Botany', were opened to the public.

Opposite below: It is sad to relate that both these galleries suffered serious damage in the bombing of Bristol in 1941 and have since been dismantled. The exhibits were largely salvaged and are now housed in the basement of the City Museum and Art Gallery. They form the nucleus of the finest natural history collection in the west of England.

Above: Mr J.W. Stagg, the Ashton Court Clerk of Works, was furnished with a motor car, to no doubt facilitate his many journeys along the roads of north Somerset to inspect Smyth farms for dilapidations. Here he is with a dog and his daughters Isabel and Ethel, who are in the back seat.

Left: Gilbert Irby indulged in a number of small cars – this one distinctly reminiscent of a governess cart – mainly for shooting. He always drove himself, usually back-to-back with two beaters. Sylvia looks about seven or eight years old, making the date of this photograph around 1907.

In loving memory of
DAME EMILY FRANCES SMYTH
Eldest daughter of the Revd Henry
Hugh Way of Alderbourne Manor
Co Bucks and widow of Sir John
Henry Greville Smyth Bart. of Ashton
Court in this Parish. This monument is
erected by her daughter Esme Smyth
Born Dec 17th 1835
she fell asleep Nov 23rd 1914

Emily Smyth died of pneumonia in the suite permanently reserved for her at her favourite hotel, Bucklands, in London, on 27 November, 1914. It was the end of an age. The First World War had begun in August. The servant problem had become acute. The Bedminster and Ashton Vale coalfields, the source of much Smyth wealth, were closed down following industrial action in 1912. The introduction of death duties meant that Esme was forced to pay over a million pounds before she could inherit. Emily was buried beside her husband in Long Ashton churchyard and a wall monument was placed to her memory in the chancel of the church.

Above: The commandant of Ashton Court hospital was Miss Araminta Bryant – a martinet who terrified staff and patients alike. The quartermaster was Miss Cashmere and the lady superintendent was Miss Morgan. There were two medical officers, Dr Newsome and Dr Pride, four trained sisters, four certified masseuses and seven night orderlies.

Opposite above: Sylvia is picking primroses for the Red Cross in Tickenham Woods, 1915. Standing, from left to right: Esme's chauffeur, a friend, Mr Froud (gamekeeper), Mrs James (housekeeper), Mrs Smyth's secretary. Sitting, from left to right: Miss Kate Hilder (lady's maid), Sylvia, Edgar Way (house steward), Miss Helen Dawe (superintendent of the Hill House Home). This was closed around 1914 and the funds went to a home for Belgian refugees in London. It is interesting that the photograph is signed 'E. Smyth'. Esme Irby was obliged to change her name in order to inherit the estate in 1914. Gilbert resented becoming a Smyth and began to distance himself from the estate and an increasingly eccentric and unpredictable wife.

Opposite below: In 1917, Esme Smyth removed her household to Ness Castle near Inverness, handed Ashton Court to the Red Cross and gave £1,200 for its conversion to a hospital for convalescent officers. The Long Gallery, which is seen here, was a designated ward for leg cases. The study became the commandant's office and some fifteen wards were created out of bedrooms on the south front. On 13 May 1917, thirty-eight cases were admitted. In less than a month, the total was 115. There were beds for 125, and a further ten for emergencies. In the first year alone, 553 were treated.

Above: Most of the medical staff lived in and eight local girls were engaged on a daily basis to work in the laundry.

Left: This is a rare photograph of one of the wards. After the war, only the neurological and shell-shocked cases remained and Esme Smyth permitted the Ministry of Pensions to continue to use Ashton Court for these cases until 1923.

Opposite below: Nerve cases are relaxing on the terrace outside the Long Gallery *c*.1920. Esme took a deep interest in 'her hospital' and made several visits to the staff and patients. In her old age she suffered a severe guilt complex about the question mark over her birth and inheritance and, by way of expiation, extended her charity to nobly born girls suffering from the stigma of illegitimacy and insanity. Ness Castle in the 1920s and Ashton Court in the 1930s were full of her pathetic protégés, who were treated alternately with great kindness and shafts of sarcasm and cruelty.

Above: The wounded officers were, for the most part, young, high-spirited and had been to university. Among them was C.S. Lewis, who later became the famous author and theologian. They produced their own magazine called *The Safety Pin*, which inevitably poked fun at 'Minnie' Bryant, and the VADs (Voluntary Aid Detachment nurses).

From 1915 to 1935, Esme Smyth lived at Ness Castle near Inverness. Here Esme threw herself into war work, organizing fundraising activities and work parties making clothes for the forces. Scarcely a week passed in the summer months without a garden party at Ness Castle for the wounded and war widows. Ness Castle had a grand entrance, but that was all. Its builder ran out of funds so it was never finished. Its merit in Esme's eyes was that all the living rooms and bedrooms were on the ground floor. In her old age, she became increasingly lame with severely ulcerated legs and could not manage stairs. The servants and guests had to 'make do' with the basement.

After the First World War, Esme sent Sylvia to a finishing school in Paris, but hearing of her amorous but entirely innocent attachment to a young American journalist, she snatched Sylvia away and forced her into a loveless marriage with Flag Lieutenant Evan Cavendish, the son of the second Baron Chesham. His mother was desperate to find a rich heiress to marry her second son, who, despite his illustrious connections with the Dukes of Devonshire and naval rank, was not thought to have many prospects.

The wedding took place at St Paul's Knightsbridge on 28 January 1923 and the cream of London society were invited. There could be no reception at Ashton Court, which was still a hospital, so the family received their guests at Claridges Hotel in Brook Street, where Esme had a permanent suite of rooms. However, on the Saturday before the wedding, Esme and Gilbert gave an 'at home' in the church home, Long Ashton, in which farm tenants, estate workers, school children and their teachers could pay their respects and tender the usual collection of Sheffield plate bric-a-brac. A revealing photograph of the last family event in the house of Smyth was taken outside church house.

Right: Susan and Greville Adrian, *c.*1930. By this time, their parents' marriage was falling apart. Evan wanted a smart wife who could entertain his important naval friends with sophisticated meals and scintillating conversation. Sylvia could not boil an egg or make a cup of tea – she had always had servants to do that. All she wanted to do was to walk her dogs in Leigh Woods.

Below: Gilbert Irby's last years were spent at Moryn, a tiny stone coastguard's cottage on the desolate east coast of Anglesey. Here he recruited local labour to rebuild the jetty and revive coastal trade. It was opened by Princess Victoria in 1926, but the project failed. He fell seriously ill in 1939. Esme visited him briefly and was there when the Second World War broke out. He died in 1940 and was buried at Hedsor, leaving his money to his Irby nephews. Never a willing Smyth, the Irbys in the end won him back.

Opposite below: The first home of commander and Mrs Cavendish was the bungalow that Greville Smyth had built for his natural history collection (which is now Redwood country club and hotel). Here, their two children were born: Susan in 1925 and Greville Adrian in 1926. Old 'Nana' Bowers who had been Sylvia's nanny, was engaged to help with the babies. The birth of a son and heir, the first in four generations, was a cause for rejoicing.

Left: Esme became increasingly quirky in her old age. She was surrounded by sycophantic poor relations, whom she indulged and bullied in turns. She could be recklessly generous one moment, ordering hundreds of dresses for her protégées, then mean and sarcastic the next. This is an amazing photograph of her romping with the gentlemen on the steps of Ness Castle.

Below: Esme took a great interest in Gaelic society and learnt to greet her Scottish servants in that language. She even managed to induce David Lloyd-George, who is here with Gilbert (on the right) to open the Ness Castle Fête in 1928. The famous battered felt hat that went into Dears Knightsbridge once a year for a new trimming can also be seen. The staff used to fall about, saying 'The museum piece has been in again'.

Esme was finding it increasingly costly to keep two great houses and reluctantly gave up Ness Castle and returned to Ashton Court in 1937. Enormous efforts had been made to return the mansion to its pre-war state and, on 16 June, Mr Charles Woodward, the caretaker, proudly hoisted the Smyth flag for the Lady's homecoming. The first days were chaotic: no fires had been lit and, while Esme and her companion Dolly Fitzway, huddled over a slow combustion stove, the Pekinese ran everywhere. The servants, now much reduced in numbers, struggled to establish some kind of order. No one could have foreseen it at the time, but the return heralded the finale in the drama of the house of Smyth.

Left: Dolly Fitzway was distantly related to Esme. She was very square and mannish, evidently had expectations and was terrified of rivals for the affections of 'milady'. Dolly often wore naval costume (her father Edgar Way had been a ship's purser) and she used to salute the 'captain', as she called Esme. Esme called her 'Squibs' and probably tolerated her secretly smoking up the chimney. Dolly is in the centre and the other lady is her friend, Wendy.

Below: Esme brought her old friend, Hector Patterson, down from Inverness to photograph Ashton Court in its final days as a stately home. His magnificent studies are now the only pictorial record of the interior, which in 1947 was stripped of its treasures and gutted. This is the alcove in the music room, which was formerly Greville Smyth's museum and is now the restaurant.

The photographs are deceptive. The superb furnishings of the restored Long Gallery conceal fundamental structural defects. In 1933, Mr Stone, Clerk of Works, reported leaks in the Winter Garden roof, burst pipes in the music room, broken cords in the sash windows, deficient water cisterns, blocked gutters, dangerous chimneys and a major crisis when the stucco ceiling of the Long Gallery started coming away from the floor above. At about this time, the north-west wing containing the billiard room and nursery quarters above, were in such a dilapidated state that they were taken out of service.

Esme had a gentleman who came to play the organ once a week, even when she was absent in Scotland for months at a time. The poor man suffered terribly from the cold, but the instrument, a three-manual organ with thirty stops, had to be kept in trim. In the great auction of 1947 it went to Hanham Baptist Chapel, where sadly it perished in a fire ten years later. In front of the organ is the magnificent screen embroidered by Emily Smyth. It is still in the family.

The entrance to the Winter Garden from the vaulted hall on the south front. In Esme's time there were love birds and parrots here. Esme had one of them destroyed because the footmen taught it bad language. The butler, Mr Reynolds, was forever calling 'Gordon, Gordon' for the hall-boy, Gordon Morgan. The servants were convulsed to hear the parrot shrieking 'Gordon, Gordon' at Esme's smart visitors.

Esme is photographing her prize bull, *c*.1939. Every June, for years, she and Lord Boston went touring to photograph Yorkshire Abbeys or the Lake District, with Ernest Roger as chauffeur. Rogers helped her with her photographic equipment and even helped her undress. He later gained a hold over her, which was much rescinded by her family and the other servants. The tours ceased abruptly when they arrived at a hotel where there was only a double bed available. Lord Boston suggested they share it. However, the photography went on and some of her studies were exhibited in the Paris Salon.

Esme's last years were spent largely in the music room, painting wooden boxes, preoccupied with Barbola work. These were sold for charity and inflicted on her friends at Christmas ad infinitum. She became increasingly absent minded and was forever sticking the wrong end of her brush in her hair and her maids had a frightful job removing the paint.

Esme and her estate agent, Bertram Worrall, quarrelled irrevocably with Evan Cavendish about the future of the estate. After the final row Esme disowned her daughter Sylvia, who by this time had left her husband, become a Roman Catholic (the estate could not be inherited by a Catholic) and fled to a cottage in the New Forest with a lady friend. Esme turned more and more to her servants and dogs for company. The dogs, which were mostly Pekinese, had individual Ming bowls and quilt coverlets, their own kennel-maids, walks and holidays and were even introduced to visitors as if they were royalty. The dogs on holiday even wrote postcards to the dogs at Ashton Court! One dated 1939 and posted in Weston-super-Mare, was addressed to 'Mathew Smyth, Ashton Court'. Mathew's grave can still be seen in the dogs' necropolis below the lawn on the south front.

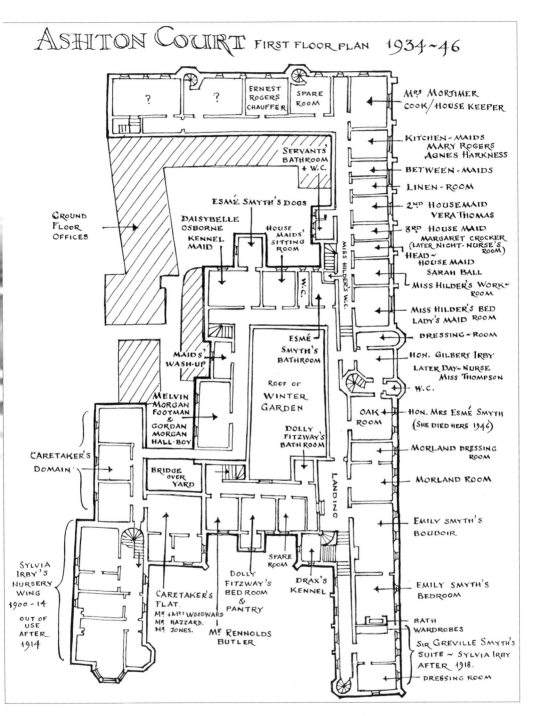

ASHTON COURT FIRST FLOOR PLAN 1934~46

Room labels on plan:

- ? ?
- ERNEST ROGERS CHAUFFER
- SPARE ROOM
- SERVANTS' BATHROOM + W.C.
- GROUND FLOOR OFFICES
- ESMÉ SMYTH'S DOGS
- DAISYBELLE OSBORNE KENNEL MAID
- HOUSE MAIDS' SITTING ROOM
- MISS HILDER'S W.C.
- W.C.
- MAIDS' WASH-UP
- ESMÉ SMYTH'S BATHROOM
- ROOF OF WINTER GARDEN
- MELVIN MORGAN FOOTMAN & GORDAN MORGAN HALL-BOY
- DOLLY FITZWAY'S BATH ROOM
- CARETAKER'S DOMAIN
- BRIDGE OVER YARD
- OAK ROOM
- LANDING
- SYLVIA IRBY'S NURSERY WING 1900-14 OUT OF USE AFTER 1914
- CARETAKER'S FLAT. Mr +Mrs WOODWARD Mr HAZZARD. Mr JONES.
- DOLLY FITZWAY'S BED ROOM & PANTRY
- Mr RENNOLDS BUTLER
- SPARE ROOM
- DRAX'S KENNEL

Right-side labels:

- Mrs MORTIMER COOK / HOUSE KEEPER
- KITCHEN-MAIDS MARY ROGERS AGNES HARKNESS
- BETWEEN-MAIDS
- LINEN-ROOM
- 2ND HOUSEMAID VERA THOMAS
- 3RD HOUSE MAID MARGARET CROCKER (LATER NIGHT-NURSE'S ROOM)
- HEAD~HOUSE MAID SARAH BALL
- MISS HILDER'S WORK~ROOM
- MISS HILDER'S BED ROOM LADY'S MAID
- DRESSING~ROOM
- HON. GILBERT IRBY
- LATER DAY-NURSE MISS THOMPSON
- W.C.
- HON. MRS ESMÉ SMYTH (SHE DIED HERE 1946)
- MORLAND DRESSING ROOM
- MORLAND ROOM
- EMILY SMYTH'S BOUDOIR
- EMILY SMYTH'S BEDROOM
- BATH WARDROBES
- SIR GREVILLE SMYTH'S SUITE ~ SYLVIA IRBY AFTER 1918.
- DRESSING ROOM

The first floor at Ashton Court was completely gutted in around 1960 because the great timber ceiling of the music room was in imminent danger of collapse. No plan of the rooms existed, but on 22 October 1989, Vera Mace, who had been second housemaid at Ashton Court from 1934 to 1946, returned to the scene of her labours and her remarkable memory has made this reconstruction possible.

Within a fortnight of the outbreak of the Second World War, Ashton Court was requisitioned by the war office as a transit camp for units from the Midlands embarking at Avonmouth. The house was surrounded by thirty-six Nissen huts, barrage balloons soared over the park and an ack-ack gun position was set up on the slopes above. Ashton Court was in the flight path of enemy bombers heading for Filton. Esme refused to leave. She had a loaded revolver placed on her work table. 'If they come,' she said, 'I shall defend my home'. Every time a bomb fell in the park she had Reynolds the butler indicate the exact spot with a black headed pin. On Friday evenings, Esme had her wheelchair pushed into the Long Gallery where dances were organised for the officers billeted in the house. In the weeks before D-Day in 1944, thousands of tanks and jeeps, all camouflaged and bearing code numbers, were marshalled under the trees in Ashton Park. From there they went straight to the Normandy beaches.

Right: The Hon. Mrs Esme Smyth (pronounced Smith) which is how she liked to be addressed, died on 1 May 1946. She was eighty-two. The funeral was a small private affair. The coffin was placed on a hay cart and brought to the church by a large black horse. The servants and estate workers turned out in force, but there were very few friends and no close relatives. She asked for Tennyson's 'Crossing the Bar' to be sung:

> '*Oh let there be no moaning at the bar*
> *When I put out to sea...*'

Below: The death of Esme Smyth brought an end to the Ashton Court Estate as a private realm. Her grandson and heir, Greville Adrian Cavendish, was barely twenty and was in the navy. The Town and Country Planning Act meant that Ashton Park was compulsorily purchased for use by the public. Greville Cavendish and his wife, Hazel, decided it was quite impracticable to live in Ashton Court. They collected a few trinkets, and the treasures of 400 years were auctioned in 1947 to pay death duties.

Opposite below: The last photograph of Esme who is in extreme old age, *c.*1945. Her world had shrunk to a corner of the music room. She weighed seventeen stone and Reynolds the butler and Rogers the chauffeur had the greatest difficulty getting her up the circular stone stairs to the Oak Room where she slept. Her staff was reduced to a mere handful. From right to left: Elsie Mortimer (cook), Isabella Thompson (nurse), Vera Mace (housemaid), Dolly Fitzway (companion), Daisy Belle Osborne (kennel maid), Arthur Reynolds (butler), Kate Hilder (lady's maid), Mr Thompson (secretary).

The servants and kitchen wing were in such a dilapidated state that in the 1960s the city council had them demolished. The loss of the kitchen wing and the disturbance to its foundations by the construction of modern buildings is regrettable, because here lay the secrets of the early evolution of the house. The extension of the service wing eastwards in the fourteenth century represents the first stage in the transformation of a medieval hall into a courtyard, enclosed by curtain walls and gatehouses.

Opposite above: For some years after 1947, Ashton Court remained unoccupied. The gardens returned to nature. Vandals broke in and stripped lead off the roofs and took what fittings remained after the sale. A vixen burrowed a lair under the library floor and reared her young there. Rain cascaded through the roof and grass grew in the long gallery.

Opposite below: The west front is boarded up. The city council finally purchased the house from Greville Cavendish in 1959, but its fate hung in the balance. These were the years before conservation and listed buildings and, it is estimated that ten mansions the size of Ashton Court were demolished every month in the 1950s.

Above: The servants' quarters from the east around 1960, showing the turret from which a bell summoned estate workers to the 'bothy' for their customary glasses of ale.

Below: The roof of the footmen's dormitory, above the medieval kitchens, which were demolished around 1860.

Above and below: The interior. The Long Gallery and Dame Emily's boudoir above suffered from massive subsidence and damp. The stucco roof fell, but most of the panelling that was removed in the 1960s still survives and hopefully will be restored one day.

Above: Between 1974 and 1976, Councillor Abraham and the BristolCity Council made the courageous decision to make the external fabric of Ashton Court watertight. Over £2 million was spent renewing the roofs and chimneys and thoroughly drying out the interior.

Right: The only inhabitant of Ashton Court in the 1960s and '70s was Mr Ivor Morris, the Lord Mayor's coachman, and his family. They lived in the flat over the stable block where the famous horses and carriages that were used on grand civic occasions were housed. They were much admired by local people, but the economic blizzard of the 1970s hastened the demise of this ancient tradition.

Left: Since the 1960s, Ashton Park has become a popular venue for large scale festivals, agricultural shows, senior citizens' days and balloon festivals regularly draw thousands of people. Part of the ground floor of the house has been restored and is open for public functions and there are ambitious plans for the extension of the visitors' centre in the stable block. At the time of writing (2003), the Long Gallery, Billiard Room and the whole of the first floor remain derelict, but there is no doubt that these will be restored when money becomes available.

Below: The future of Ashton Court as a multicultural and leisure centre for the people of Bristol is assured. Lottery funding, which was approved in 2003, will permit the first stage in the restoration of the gardens and park. It is hoped that collaboration with the private sector will ultimately find a user who will combine a modern function for the interior and sensitive restoration of its architectural heritage.

Other local titles published by Tempus

Bishopsworth, Withywood and Hartcliffe

ANTON BANTOCK AND THE MALAGO SOCIETY

These images of Bishopsworth's past tell the stories of the once isolated north Somerset village and its surrounding farmland and how the area has grown to include the housing estates of Hartcliffe and Withywood. Each double page opens a different window on the history of a community which is typical of so many others, but unique in its own personalities and stories.
0 7524 0689 2

Bristol Times Revisited

DAVID HARRISON

Bristol Times Revisited is the second collection of some of the most remarkable articles drawn from the first year of the *Bristol Times* supplement of the *Bristol Evening Post*. Accompanied by photographs from the newspaper's archive it will serve to remind Bristol's older residents of days gone by, while revealing the unique history of the city to younger readers.
0 7524 2844 6

Castle Park Before the Blitz

MAURICE BYE

This fascinating book records life in the area of Bristol, known today as Castle Park, before it was largely destroyed during a bombing raid on the night of 24 November 1940. This unique selection documents a variety of everyday scenes well known to the those who have lived and continue to live in Bristol.
0 7524 2864 0

Bristol Channel Shipping Remembered

CHRIS COLLARD

In its heyday the Bristol Channel was a thriving estuary where ships of all descriptions were to be seen. *Bristol Channel Shipping Remembered* is a nostaligic tour of the Bristol Channel, from Bristol down to its westerly limits and then eastwards along the coast of South Wales to Newport and shows us some of these once familiar scenes that have become little more than just memories of this great waterway.
0 7524 2388 6

If you are interested in purchasing other books published by Tempus, or in case you have difficulty finding any Tempus books in your local bookshop, you can also place orders directly through our website

www.tempus-publishing.com

or from   **BOOKPOST**, Freepost, PO Box 29, Douglas, Isle of Man, IM99 1BQ
tel 01624 836000   email bookshop@enterprise.net